W9-CRM-174

Hallucinogens and Shamanism

Hallucinogens
and
Shamanism

Edited by

MICHAEL J. HARNER

OXFORD UNIVERSITY PRESS
London   Oxford   New York

Acknowledgments

Banisteriopsis caapi, p. 2. *Lloydia*, courtesy L. E. Smith

Banisteriopsis caapi and Peyote, pp. 3 and 60. Courtesy R. E. Schultes, Botanical Museum of Harvard University

Jívaro Shaman, pp. 18 and 19. Photographs by Michael Harner

Campa Shaman, p. 42. Courtesy Gerald Weiss

Deadly Nightshade, p. 126. Edith G. Wheelwright, *The Physick Garden*, 1934. New York Public Library

Henbane, Mandrake, Thorn Apple, pp. 126 and 127. Pierandrea Matioli, *Commentaries on the Six Books of Dioscorides*, 1563. Reproduced from Joseph Wood Krutch, *Herbal*, 1965. Courtesy G. P. Putnam's Sons

Departure for the Sabat, p. 136. Queverdo, engraved by Maleuvre. New York Public Library

Hexenküche, p. 137. Kunsthistoriches Museum, Vienna

Witches on a Pitchfork, p. 142. Ulrich Molitor, *De Laniis et phitonicus mulieribus*. New York Public Library

Cocina des las brujas, p. 143. Mas-Art Reference Bureau

Sketches on pages 161, 170–71, collected by Michael Harner

Sketches on pages 186–87, collected by Claudio Naranjo

Sketch of a boa constrictor, p. 170. *The Jívaro: People of the Sacred Waterfalls*, by Michael J. Harner, © 1972 by Michael J. Harner. Reproduced by permission of Doubleday & Company, Inc.

A certain Frenchman in his Book called Daemonomania, *Tearms me a Magician, a Conjurer, and thinks this Book of mine, long since Printed, worthy to be burnt, because I have written the Fairies Oyntment, which I set forth onely in detestation of the frauds of Divels and Witches; That which comes by Nature is abused by their superstition, which I borrowed from the Books of the most commendable Divines. . . . I pass over other men of the same temper, who affirm that I am a Witch and a Conjurer, whereas I never writ here nor elsewhere, what is not contain'd within the bounds of Nature.*

Giovanni Porta, Natural Magick, 1658, *preface*

Preface

THE recent surge of interest in hallucinogenic agents in our own culture is beginning to contribute to a greatly increased awareness in anthropology of the role of such substances in other societies. Although anthropologists have long been interested in the function of the peyote cactus (*Lophophora williamsii*) in North American Indian cultures (e.g., Aberle, 1966; La Barre, 1938, 1960), they have generally tended to neglect the ethnological importance of other natural hallucinogens, such as the psychotropic mushrooms and certain of the solanaceous plants (species of the potato family), as well as the theoretical importance of the subject as a whole. Thus, some of the most significant contributions have been made not by anthropologists, but by pharmacologists such as Lewin (1964 [orig. 1924]), and botanists such as Schultes (e.g., 1940, 1955) and Wasson (e.g., 1961, and Wasson and Wasson, 1957).*

Undoubtedly one of the major reasons that anthropologists for so long underestimated the importance of hallucinogenic substances in shamanism and religious experience was that very few had partaken themselves of the native psychotropic materials (other than peyote) or had undergone the resulting subjective experiences so critical, perhaps paradoxically, to an empirical understanding of their meaning to the peoples they studied. Most, although not all, of the authors in the present book are an excep-

---

* For brief surveys of hallucinogenic plant use from the viewpoint of botany and pharmacognosy, see Schultes (1963) and Farnsworth (1968). More recently, since the completion of the present work, two books have been published emphasizing an anthropological perspective (Dobkin de Rios, 1972; and Furst, 1972).

tion, and the majority of the articles are by younger anthropologists describing the results of their recent, first-hand field research. These contributions are intended as a small step toward rectifying the hitherto inadequate attention native hallucinogens have received in anthropology.

M.J.H.

New York
Autumn 1972

Contents

Introduction

THE use of hallucinogenic agents to achieve trance states for perceiving and contacting the supernatural world is evidently an ancient and widespread human practice. In using a powerful hallucinogen, an individual is brought face to face with visions and experiences of an overwhelming nature, tending strongly to reinforce his beliefs in the reality of the supernatural world. We of a literate civilization may get both our religion and our religious proofs from books; persons in non-literate societies often rely upon direct confrontation with the supernatural for evidence of religious reality.

In non-literate societies, the experts who directly confront the supernatural are called "shamans" by anthropologists. Shaman, a term preferred in anthropology partially because it lacks the sensational or negative connotation of "witch" or "witch-doctor," is a word from the language of the Tungus tribe of Siberia. A shaman may be defined as a man or woman who is in direct contact with the spirit world through a trance state and has one or more spirits at his command to carry out his bidding for good or evil. Typically shamans bewitch persons with the aid of spirits or cure persons made ill by other spirits, whether sent by another shaman or simply acting on their own volition. Depending on his traditions and beliefs, a shaman may also influence the course of events, find lost or stolen objects, divine the identity of persons who have committed crimes, communicate with the spirits of dead relatives and friends of clients, foretell the future, and practice clairvoyance. Contemporary anthropology tends to view the shaman as a psychotherapist, but the people of the cultures in which he operates believe him to be able to contact and deal with an invisible spirit world. In most non-literate societies the shaman is accorded considerable respect.

The use of psychedelic agents is only one of the ways of achieving the trance-like states conducive to a sense of seeing and contacting the supernatural. In many cultures other methods are used: fasting (water and food); flagellation and self-torture; sensory deprivation; breathing exercises and yogic meditation; and ritual dancing and drumming. A common psycho-physiological basis for the similarity of effects produced by all of these methods may exist, but the use of hallucinogens appears to be the easiest and fastest technique for reaching a believed supernatural experience and visions.

One of the most typical aspects of the shamanistic experience is the change into another state of consciousness, often called a trance, with the shaman feeling that he is taking a journey. During the past few years it has become common to speak of "taking a trip" with a psychedelic substance, and this is no coincidence. A shaman on a "trip" or journey typically passes through situations involving spirits, often hostile, and often belonging to other shamans, with whom he has to deal in order to cure an illness or to bewitch someone with his own spirits.

Any discussion of hallucinogens and shamanism must consider the relationship between the two in northeast Asia—the home of what has been commonly termed "classic" shamanism, i.e., as practiced by the native Siberians and the first to be described in detail in the ethnological literature. In this region we find a close relationship between the psychoactive mushroom, fly-agaric (*Amanita muscaria*), and the shamanistic act. *Amanita muscaria* is known to contain muscarine and muscimol, both with demonstrated hallucinogenic properties, as well as other psychotropic substances in limited quantities or of undetermined effects (Eugster, 1967; Waser, 1967).

In Siberia, *Amanita* was used by shamans and others in the Koryak, Chukchi, Yukagir, Yakut, Ostyak, Samoyed, and Kamchadal tribes. Jochelson (1905–1908: 583), who traveled among the Koryak in 1900–1901, writes:

. . . fly-agaric produces intoxication, hallucinations, and delirium. Light forms of intoxication are accompanied by a certain degree of animation and some spontaneity of movements. Many shamans, previous to their seances, eat fly-agaric to get into ecstatic states. . . . Under strong intoxication the senses become de-

Fly agaric (*Amanita muscaria*)

ranged; surrounding objects appear either very large or very small, hallucinations set in, spontaneous movements and convulsions. So far as I could observe, attacks of great animation alternate with moments of deep depression. The person intoxicated by fly-agaric sits quietly rocking from side to side, even taking part in conversations with his family. Suddenly his eyes dilate, he begins to gesticulate convulsively, converses with persons whom he imagines he sees, sings, and dances. Then an interval of rest sets in again. However, to keep up the intoxication additional doses of fungi are necessary. . . . There is reason to think that the effect of fly-agaric would be stronger were not its alkaloid quickly taken out of the organism with the urine. The Koryak knows this by experience, and the urine of persons intoxicated with fly-agaric is not wasted. The drunkard himself drinks it to prolong his hallucinations, or he offers it to others as a treat.

The theoretical literature has largely overlooked the fact that even this "classic" shamanism often involved the use of hallucinogen. Thus one can read entire books on shamanism or primitive religion without finding any reference to hallucinogens except for peyote. Yet by patient library research one can find overwhelming evidence of the use of such substances in connection with the supernatural in scores of cultures. We are now beginning to see such research undertaken and, perhaps of more urgent importance, anthropologists are starting to pursue field investigations on the use of native hallucinogens other than peyote, as the contents of this volume demonstrate.

With such work, long-standing controversies over the personality and psychopathology of shamans will undoubtedly benefit from a serious consideration of the potentiality of native psychedelics to temporarily transport almost any individual to another state of consciousness. Discussions of world view and supernatural belief systems may also be expected to profit from an investigation of the extent to which these substances are used in religious rites and vision quests. There can be little doubt that the use of the more powerful hallucinogens tends to strongly reinforce a belief in the reality of the supernatural world and in the existence of a disembodied soul or souls. An intriguing possibility is that hallucinogenic experiences may have also played a role in the innovation of such beliefs. This is an important question which clearly deserves comprehensive cross-cultural and inter-disciplinary research.

The social implications of the use of hallucinogens may also prove to be significant in a variety of cultures. The widespread utilization of such substances in a population to obtain direct revelations very probably tends to compete with the authority of priestly hierarchies. The authority of shamans themselves as special agents of contact with the supernatural has been reported threatened by the general adoption of peyote in two societies (Slotkin, 1956:47; Boyer *et al.*, in this volume). Conversely, we may expect to discover that certain types of social structures are more conducive than others to the development of conditions leading to widespread hallucinogen use.

Finally, as more anthropologists undertake field research on the significance of hallucinogens and partake of the drugs themselves (e.g., Castaneda 1968; 1971), it will be interesting to see how "participant observation" influences their understanding of the cultures studied and affects their personal, theoretical, and methodological orientations.

The reader will find that the New World is overwhelmingly emphasized as a region of research in the following pages. There are several reasons for this, not the least of which is that in recent times little anthropological research on the use of hallucinogens in shamanism has been undertaken anywhere else. Also, as Schultes (1963: 147) has pointed out, the New World is unusually rich in hallucinogenic plants, a factor which undoubtedly facilitated their use by North American Indians, but especially by Middle and South American Indians. Finally, the Western hemisphere is also one of the best regions of the world, along with aboriginal Siberia, for the study of shamanism in general. For reasons that are not entirely clear, the American Indian cultures have often preserved an emphasis on shamanism, perhaps because the overwhelming majority were untrammeled by a state religion. Today similar circumstances are usually found only in the most remote parts of the Old World.

It is not claimed here that hallucinogenic plants were used in shamanistic practices in all, or even most, cultures. However, it is proposed that the importance of such plants, where their use existed, frequently has been overlooked. Anthropologists are not free of ethnocentrism; too often, like explorers and missionaries, they have passed over the significance of some unidentified "noxious herb" that the people they were visiting "claimed" to use to get into a trance state. Now that such drugs have come to our own contemporary culture, we are more prepared to see the significance of their use elsewhere. One cannot help but wonder what other aspects of knowledge acquired in other times and places remain essentially invisible to us.

I

In the Primitive World: The Upper Amazon

ONE of the last remaining areas of the world where hallucinogenic drugs are used under essentially aboriginal conditions is the upper Amazon rain forest of South America. The four papers in this section are all based upon work among the American Indian tribes of that area, where shamanistic practices typically involve the ingestion of a hallucinogenic tea or brew made from the *Banisteriopsis* vine.

The drink, commonly called *yagé* or *yajé* in Colombia, *ayahuasca* (Quechua: "vine of the dead") in Ecuador and Peru, and *caapi* in Brazil, appears to be prepared, in part at least, always from one of the several known species of *Banisteriopsis*, a genus belonging to the *Malpighiaceae*, or from genera closely related to *Banisteriopsis*. Discussions of the progress and problems in botanical identification may be found in Schultes (1957, 1963), Friedberg (1965), and Pinkley (1969).

The distribution of the native use of *Banisteriopsis* is at present known to be from northwestern Colombia in the north to lowland Bolivia in the south, occurring both east and west of the Andes, and extending eastward into the upper Orinoco area. The plant has also been reported from British Guiana and from as far east as Pará, Brazil, at the mouth of the Amazon (Morton, 1930:158), but it is not clear if the Indians from those areas have utilized it.

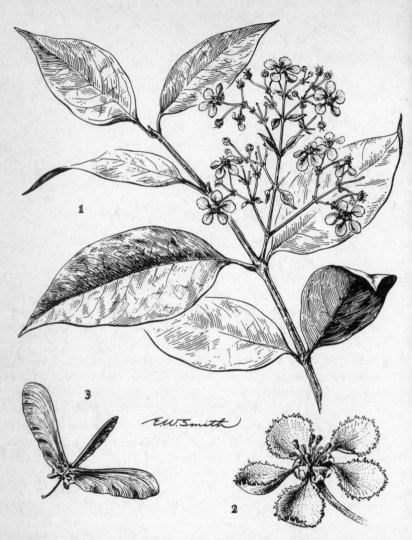

Banisteriopsis caapi, one of the two plants commonly used in preparing the brew known as *yagé*, *ayahuasca*, *caapi*, or among the Jívaro, *natemä*

Banisteriopsis caapi cultivated by Barasana Indians. Río Piraparaná, Comisaría del Vaupés, Colombia

Banisteriopsis species exist throughout Central America and Mexico, including the Yucatan Peninsula, and at least one species is reported from the southeastern United States (Standley and Steyermark, 1946:472), but use has apparently not been recorded in those areas.

All members of the genus grow wild as tree-climbing forest vines, but some tribes cultivate the plants in their gardens as well as collecting them in the wild state. A variety of other plants may be boiled together with *Banisteriopsis*, depending upon the tribe. Typically, however, only one other plant is added to the brew. Spruce (1908: 415), who originally made the botanical identification of *Banisteriopsis*, reported that a "twiner of the

genus *Haemadictyon*" (now called *Prestonia* [Schultes, 1960:
172]), was employed as the second plant among the Indians of
the Rio Negro region in Brazil. He noted that they considered it
essential to the success of the drink. Among the Cofan, Inga, and
Sione Indians of the Río Putumayo area of eastern Colombia,
Schultes (1960:176) found that the second plant was simply a
second species of *Banisteriopsis*. Another botanist, García-Barriga,
reporting on the preparation of the drink in the same region,
states that two other plants were added, one of the genus *Al-
tenanthera* and the other unidentified (Schultes, 1960:176). In
the Río Napo region slightly to the south, Hochstein and Paradies
report that *Prestonia* is added to the preparation (Schultes, 1960:
176).

More recently, *Psychotria viridis*, containing the powerful hallucinogen N,N-dimethyltryptamine, has been identified as an
admixture regularly used by the Cofan Indians in eastern Ecuador
(Pinkley, 1969) and by the Cashinahua of eastern Peru, who call
it *nai kawa* (Der Marderosian, Kensinger, Chao, and Goldstein,
1970). On the Río Ucayali in eastern Peru, I found that the
Shipibo-Conibo also add to *ayahuasca* the leaves of a botanically
unidentified plant called *cawa*, which presumably is the *Psychotria*
of the linguistically related Cashinahua. Carneiro also reports (unpublished field notes) that the neighboring and closely related
Amahuaca Indians use *kawa* leaves as a strengthener. Other plants
used by the Amahuaca in the *Banisteriopsis* brew are *chuchupawa*,
cha'i, and *chuchupano* (Carneiro, 1964: 8; unpublished field notes).
Cha'i is sometimes drunk first, before taking *ayahuasca*, to increase
the hallucinations.

Without attempting to review all the literature, the observation
may be made that the common denominator in the drinks called
yagé, *caapi*, or *ayahuasca* is *Banisteriopsis*. Although the *Banisteriopsis* brew may be taken alone, it is commonly believed among
the Indians that adding one or more of several different kinds of
plants to the mixture provides added strength.

The biochemistry of *Banisteriopsis* drinks, particularly because
of the variety of admixtures involved, is not well known, as
Schultes (1960: 177–79; 1970: 576–77) has observed. The alkaloid
harmine has been known for some time to be a constituent; more

recently harmaline and d-tetrahydroharmine, also alkaloids, have been found in *Banisteriopsis caapi* by Hochstein and Paradies (Schultes, 1960:179). Now it also appears that *Banisteriopsis rusbyana*, sometimes mixed with one of the other *Banisteriopsis* species, contains significant amounts of the fast-acting hallucinogenic alkaloid N,N-dimethyltryptamine (Poisson, 1965; Agurell *et al.*, 1968; Der Marderosian *et al.*, 1968). There exists little, if any, information on the alkaloid constituents of complete brews embodying two or more plants. The four aforementioned alkaloids known to be present are structurally related indole derivatives and, as such, are related to the well-known hallucinogens mescaline (found in peyote), psilocybin (found in the psychotropic Mexican mushroom), and LSD (lysergic acid diethylamide tartrate).

Typically, *Banisteriopsis* is taken by South American Indian shamans of the tropical forest in order to perceive the supernatural world and to contact and to affect the behavior of particular supernatural entities, as in locating and withdrawing a supernatural object from a bewitched patient. In many tribes, non-shamans, most commonly males, also take *ayahuasca* for such reasons as to obtain information with the help of the spirit world, to obtain visions, to achieve supernatural power, or to accompany a shaman in a curing or other ritual. Depending upon the culture and the purpose, the person taking *Banisteriopsis* may drink the mixture alone or as a member of a group. Thus, the individualistic and feuding Jívaro prefer to take the drug individually and to use it to cope supernaturally with enemies. The more gregarious Cashinahua and Sharanahua, on the other hand, tend to participate together in the hallucinogenic experience and to share those aspects of the revelatory content which hold portents for the common good of the group. The Campa also join together for *Banisteriopsis* sessions, but their shaman plays a directorial role as leader of the ceremonies. All four groups illustrate how hallucinogenic experiences may be deeply integrated into the supernatural life and total culture of a people. More specifically, they shed light on the shamanistic function of hallucinogens in societies which have not yet been significantly altered by Westernization.

In his paper on the Cashinahua of eastern Peru, Kensinger shows how a hallucinogen can permit almost all the members of a society to participate in an essentially shamanistic trance experience. He emphasizes the content of their *ayahuasca*-induced visions and sees their experiences as a source of information that they cannot obtain by ordinary means. Kensinger does not attempt to explain away the information they obtain, but rather adds his own corroboratory evidence for their belief. He also provides valuable data on the common themes of the Cashinahua hallucinogenic experience with *ayahuasca* and points up the fact that the concept of a "trip" is not peculiar to modern American psychedelic subculture. In contrast to the members of that subculture, however, the Cashinahua find hallucinogen-taking an unpleasant experience, and undergo it despite that fact in order to obtain urgently desired revelations from the spirit world. Here, as elsewhere in the primitive world, the use of hallucinogens is usually for serious supernatural purposes rather than for recreation.

My paper on the Jívaro of eastern Ecuador also indicates how the presence of the hallucinogenic *Banisteriopsis* mixture makes it possible for virtually anyone to achieve the trance state necessary for the practice of shamanism and thus contributes, along with economic and social factors (see Harner, 1972), to the high proportion of shamans in Jívaro society. The paper here focuses on the "inside view" of the shaman toward reality, a reality which is defined among the Jívaro as being capable of being seen only when one is under the influence of a hallucinogen. They see the ordinary world as misleading and "a lie." This point of view, indicative of the impressiveness of their hallucinogenically-induced experiences, has a resemblance to the viewpoint expressed by Castaneda (1968, 1971) with regard to the distinction between "ordinary" and "non-ordinary" reality. The Jívaro, however, go even further and believe that there is only one reality, the supernatural.

Siskind, in her contribution on the Sharanahua, closely related neighbors of the Cashinahua, is explicitly concerned with a problem that Castaneda raises, specifically the degree to which "consensual validation" is operative in the structuring of the hallucinatory experience. Using the case of the Sharanahua, she focuses on the communication system employed between shaman and patient while both are under the influence of the *Banisteriopsis* drink. She emphasizes the importance of cultural factors, such as traditional curing songs, in affecting the nature of the patient's experience and his belief that he has been cured. Siskind sees the patient cured through the social reintegration of the individual into the kin-oriented community with the aid of the group *ayahuasca* session guided by the shaman.

Weiss discusses the *ayahuasca*-drinking ceremony of the Campa of eastern Peru in terms of its possible evolutionary implications. He suggests that the role of the shaman as director of the ceremony may shed light on how priests may have originally developed from shamans. Implicitly, his paper also raises questions about the possible use of hallucinogens in early priesthoods. Such drugs, which permit the achievement of trance states by perhaps otherwise uninspired persons in appointed positions, are known to be employed by Zuñi rain priests in the southwestern United States (Stevenson, 1915: 39, 89, 90). As Wasson (1968) has suggested for India, some of the relatively innocuous "blessed sacraments" of contemporary hierarchically organized religions may have originally been hallucinogens. However, direct revelations, even when restricted to an elite few, are sooner or later bound to come into conflict with the orthodox dogma fundamental to the ideological structure of state religions, and the use of such substances apparently tends to be eventually forbidden, as in Europe (see Chapter 8).

1

Banisteriopsis *Usage Among the Peruvian Cashinahua*

Kenneth M. Kensinger

We drank *nixi pae*. Before starting to chant, we talked a bit. The brew began to move me and I drank some more. Soon I began to shake all over. The earth shook. The wind blew and the trees swayed. . . . The *nixi pae* people began to appear. They had bows and arrows and wanted to shoot me. I was afraid but they told me their arrows would not kill me, only make me more drunk. . . . Snakes, large brightly colored snakes were crawling on the ground. They began to crawl all over me. One large female snake tried to swallow me, but since I was chanting she couldn't succeed. . . . I heard armadillo tail trumpets and then many frogs and toads singing. The world was transformed. Everything became bright. I moved very fast. Not my body but my eye spirit. . . . I saw lots of gardens full of manioc and plantains. The storage sheds were full of corn. The peanut racks were full. . . . I came down the trail to a village. There was much noise, the sound of people laughing. They were dancing *kacha*, the fertility dance. Everybody was

KENNETH M. KENSINGER, M.A., is on the anthropology faculty at Bennington College, Vermont. Formerly Lecturer in Anthropology at Columbia University, New York, and once a member of the Summer Institute of Linguistics in Peru, he has spent a number of years in linguistic and ethnographic research among the Cashinahua.

laughing. Many of the women were pregnant. I was happy. I knew we would be well and have plenty to eat.[1]

This excerpt from the report of one informant illustrates the basic aspects of *Banisteriopsis* usage among the Cashinahua.[2] *Nixi pae*, "the vine drunkenness"—also known as *ayahuasca* by the local Peruvians (and the term I will use from this point on)—is prepared from the stalks of several lianas of the genus *Banisteriopsis* and the leaves of a shrub identified as a member of the genus *Psychotria*. Preliminary chemical analysis indicates that the active hallucinogenic agents of the *Banisteriopsis* are harmine and harmaline, that of the *Psychotria* is dimethyltryptamine (DMT) (Der Marderosian *et al.*, 1970).

Banisteriopsis is considered by the Cashinahua to be the basic ingredient of *ayahuasca*; and although *Psychotria* is clearly viewed as an additive, it is an important ingredient, without which the hallucinations are said to be less vivid and of shorter duration.

Any initiated Cashinahua male may drink *ayahuasca*. Usage varies widely; some men never drink it, others imbibe every time a brew is prepared. *Ayahuasca* bouts rarely occur more frequently than every other week, and then only after dark, generally beginning about eight in the evening and lasting until two or three in the morning. General consensus about the need or advisability of drinking seems to determine the timing of *ayahuasca* parties.

Although all the men know how to prepare the beverage, it normally falls to one or two men from each village to make the preparations. The host goes to the jungle and without any ritual

1. An earlier version of this paper was presented as part of the symposium Hallucinogens and Shamanism at the annual meeting of the American Anthropological Association, November 1968, in Seattle, and portions have appeared in Der Marderosian *et al.*, 1970. The data were gathered during several field trips between July 1955 and August 1968.

2. The Cashinahua, a small tribe of approximately 500 persons who live in the tropical rain forest of southeastern Peru along the Curanja River, are classified as members of the Panoan language family (McQuown, 1956:518), and of the Jurua-Purus Culture Area (Murdock, 1951:135). Additional Cashinahua live along the Jurua and Embira rivers and their tributaries in the state of Acre in western Brazil. Although I have worked with several informants from Brazil while they were visiting their Peruvian kinsmen, and the data collected from them tend to agree with that from the Peruvian Cashinahua, all data in this paper come from and refer only to the Cashinahua from the Curanja River area.

or ceremony selects and cuts one to two meters of *Banisteriopsis* and three to five branches of *Psychotria*. On returning to his house, he cuts the vine into 6- to 8-inch segments which he pounds lightly with a rock and places in a clay cooking pot with a two- to four-gallon capacity. The leaves and buds of the *Psychotria* are stripped from the branches and added to the pot which is then filled with water. A fire is lit around the base of the pot, and allowed to burn until the water nearly reaches a boil. The brew is steeped for about an hour, after which it is ladled off into smaller pots to cool.

As the hour for the affair approaches the host places some stools and logs near the hearth. Each man, when he arrives, goes to the pots and dips out about one pint of the liquid. He sings or chants several phrases over the brew, asking it to show him many things, and then gulps it down. He then joins the others and talks or chants quietly while waiting for the effects of the drug to begin. After fifteen minutes he may drink another pint, particularly if he wishes to hallucinate freely, or as the Cashinahua say, "to have a good trip." [3]

Once the drug "begins to shake them," chanting begins in earnest. Each man sings independently. Chants often involve conversations with the spirits of *ayahuasca*; at other times they merely consist of the rhythmic repetition of the monosyllabic 'e 'e· 'e· 'e 'e· 'e·. Those who do not know the chants sit next to someone who does, swaying their bodies in time with the rhythm.

Although each man operates on his own, the group is very important, as it provides him a contact with the real world, without which the terrors of the spirit world through which he is traveling could be overwhelming. Frequently a group of men will line up on a log, each one wrapping his arms and legs around the man ahead of him. Only the men who are "strong," i.e. those who have had many years of experience with *ayahuasca*, will not maintain physical contact with at least one other person. *Ayahuasca* is never taken by a person alone.

The volume of the chanting rises and falls, punctuated by

3. *Nixi paewen en bai wai pe* "Vine drunkenness-with I trip make good." The term translated "trip" (*bai*) has the idea of a sightseeing excursion with house calls for visiting.

shrieks of terror, retching, and vomiting. No attempt is made to coordinate either the rhythm or pitch of the chants. Each man devotes his attention to what he is experiencing and his own search for knowledge.

In spite of the individual nature of the hallucinogenic experience there is a high degree of similarity in the content and frequency of occurrence of particular hallucinations from individual to individual during any one night of drinking. Certain themes also recur every time they drink *ayahuasca*. The most frequent of these are: (1) brightly colored, large snakes; (2) jaguars and ocelots; (3) spirits, both of *ayahuasca* and others; (4) large trees, often falling trees; (5) lakes, frequently filled with anacondas and alligators; (6) Cashinahua villages and those of other Indians; (7) traders and their goods; and (8) gardens. All informants speak of the sense of motion and rapid change, or as they say, transformation. Particular hallucinations wax and wane, interspersed by others in a very fluid manner. There is a sense of darkness interrupted often by flashing bright colors or brightness when the horizon seems to collapse. Time and space perceptions are distorted.[4]

However, the most persistent comment about *ayahuasca* from all informants is, "It is a fearsome thing, I was very much afraid." Few informants have ever admitted that they find it a pleasant experience.

If they find it so unpleasant, so fearful, why do they persist in using the drug? The answer lies in the relevance of the hallucinations for personal action.

The Cashinahua drink *ayahuasca* in order to learn about things, persons, and events removed from them by time and/or space

4. Hallucinations generally involve scenes which are a part of the Cashinahua's daily experience. However, informants have described hallucinations about places far removed both geographically and from their own experience. Several informants who have never been to or seen pictures of Pucallpa, the large town at the Ucayali River terminus of the Central Highway, have described their visits under the influence of *ayahuasca* to the town with sufficient detail for me to be able to recognize specific shops and sights. On the day following one *ayahuasca* party six of nine men informed me of seeing the death of my *chai*, "my mother's father." This occurred two days before I was informed by radio of his death.

which could affect either the society as a whole or its individual members.

Hallucinations are viewed as the experiences of an individual's dream spirit;[5] they are portents of things to come or reminders of the past. Thus, after a night of drinking, the men discuss some of their experiences, particularly those which seem to have relevance for the society, such as visions of an abundance of food, or hunger and famine, health or sickness, and death. Although in most cases little can be done to alter events foreseen in visions, some precautions can be taken. For example, when famine is seen, gardens can be enlarged, or when a foreigner is seen coming, bringing sickness with him, they may decide to leave the village for an extended hunting trip. Such decisions will affect a man, his wife and his children, and on occasion his extended family. Rarely, however, would decisions based on information gained through *ayahuasca* affect an entire village, and never the whole society.

Ayahuasca is used on occasion to obtain information about the cause of an illness which has not responded to traditional treatments.[6] In case of sickness, a person usually tries to cure himself. When cure does not follow, an herbalist is consulted. After hearing the symptoms, he prescribes sweet medicine. Several such consultations are often required. If, after repeated tries, sweet

5. The Cashinahua believe that each person has five spirits: *bedu yuxin* "the eye spirit"—the spirit which lives in one's eyes and is the true person, his personality; *yuda bake yuxin* "the body child spirit"—one's shadow; *nama yuxin* "the dream spirit"—that part of the individual which leaves the body during sleep, intoxication, or unconsciousness, causing dreams, hallucinations, etc.; *pui yuxin* "the spirit of defecation" and *isun yuxin* "the spirit of urination."

6. The Cashinahua have two kinds of medical specialists: the herbalist, *huni bata dauya* or *huni dauya* "the man with sweet medicine" or "the man with medicine," and the shaman, *huni mukaya* "the man with bitter." The herbalist treats diseases which are caused by both natural and supernatural agents but not the result of the action of any specific spirit being. He prescribes treatment involving a multiplicity of plant remedies according to the symptoms exhibited by his patient. The shaman treats diseases thought to be caused by the action of spirit beings by replacing the causative agent with the spiritual quality or power *muka dau* which he has received from his spirit familiars in the process of becoming a shaman. The process of transfering the *muka dau* from the shaman's body to the patient is unclear (Kensinger, n.d.).

medicine fails, a shaman is consulted. He reviews the history of the case, and then consults his spirit familiars about the cause of the illness, normally an intrusive object or spirit which he then removes from the patient with a small quantity of *muka dau*, "bitter medicine" which resides in the shaman's body, and which must then be removed from the patient by the herbalist's sweet medicine. It is only when these procedures fail to produce the desired cure that the shaman resorts to *ayahuasca*. A special drinking session is called, during which the shaman consults with spirits outside his normal sphere of influence, who inform him of the cause of the illness, or a new chant which should be used along with sucking or massage, or the kind of sweet medicine to request from the herbalist, or that the illness is incurable.

In conclusion, the Cashinahua use *Banisteriopsis* as a means of gaining information not available through the normal channels of communication, which, in addition to other information, forms the basis for personal action. The shaman's usage of *ayahuasca* is merely a specific case of a more general social phenomenon in a situation where his normal methods fail.

REFERENCES

Der Marderosian, Ara H., Kenneth M. Kensinger, Jew-ming Chao, and Frederick J. Goldstein
   1970   The Use and Hallucinatory Principles of a Psychoactive Beverage of the Cashinahua Tribe (Amazon Basin). *Drug Dependence* No. 5, pp. 7–14.
Kensinger, Kenneth M.
   n.d.   *The Cashinahua Cultural Domain Dau.* An unpublished report to the Joint Committee on Latin American Studies of the Social Science Research Council and the American Council of Learned Societies.
McQuown, Norman A.
   1956   The Indigenous Languages of Latin America. *American Anthropologist* 58: 501–70.
Murdock, George Peter
   1951   *Outline of South American Cultures.* New Haven: Human Relations Area Files.

2

The Sound of Rushing Water

Michael J. Harner

He had drunk, and now he softly sang. Gradually, faint lines and forms began to appear in the darkness, and the shrill music of the tsentsak, *the spirit helpers, arose around him. The power of the drink fed them. He called, and they came. First,* pangi, *the anaconda, coiled about his head, transmuted into a crown of gold. Then* wampang, *the giant butterfly, hovered above his shoulder and sang to him with its wings. Snakes, spiders, birds and bats danced in the air above him. On his arms appeared a thousand eyes as his demon helpers emerged to search the night for enemies.*

The sound of rushing water filled his ears, and listening to its roar, he knew he possessed the power of Tsungi, the first shaman. Now he could see. Now he could find the truth. He stared at the stomach of the sick man. Slowly, it became transparent like a shallow mountain stream, and he saw within it, coiling and un-

MICHAEL J. HARNER, PH.D., is an Associate Professor of Anthropology on the Graduate Faculty of the New School for Social Research, New York, and has also taught at Columbia University, Yale University, and the University of California, Berkeley. In four expeditions to the upper Amazon rain forest, he has engaged in ethnological research among the Jívaro, Achuara, and Conibo-Shipibo Indians, all of whom utilize hallucinogenic drugs. This paper was first published in *Natural History Magazine*, Vol. 77, No. 6 (June–July), 1968, and is reprinted here by permission. Additional information on Jívaro hallucinogen use and shamanism may be found in Harner, 1972.

coiling, makanchï, *the poisonous serpent, who had been sent by the enemy shaman. The real cause of the illness had been found.*

The Jívaro Indians of the Ecuadorian Amazon believe that witchcraft is the cause of the vast majority of illnesses and non-violent deaths. The normal waking life, for the Jívaro, is simply a "lie," or illusion, while the true forces that determine daily events are supernatural and can only be seen and manipulated with the aid of hallucinogenic drugs. A reality view of this kind creates a particularly strong demand for specialists who can cross over into the supernatural world at will to deal with the forces that influence and even determine the events of the waking life.

These specialists, called "shamans" by anthropologists, are recognized by the Jívaro as being of two types: bewitching shamans or curing shamans. Both kinds take a hallucinogenic drink, whose Jívaro name is *natemä,** in order to enter the supernatural world. This brew is prepared from segments of the vine *Banisteriopsis caapi,* a species belonging to the Malpighiaceae. The Jívaro boil it with the leaves of a similar vine, which probably is also a species of *Banisteriopsis,* to produce a tea that contains the powerful hallucinogenic alkaloids harmaline, harmine, d-tetrahydroharmine, and quite possibly N,N-dimethyltryptamine (DMT) (Agurell, Holmstedt, and Lindgren, 1968; Der Marderosian, 1967: 26; Friedberg, 1965; Poisson, 1965).

When I first undertook research among the Jívaro in 1956–57, I did not fully appreciate the psychological impact of the *Banisteriopsis* drink upon the native view of reality, but in 1961 I had occasion to drink the hallucinogen in the course of field work with another Upper Amazon Basin tribe. For several hours after drinking the brew, I found myself, although awake, in a world literally beyond my wildest dreams. I met bird-headed people, as well as dragon-like creatures who explained that they were the true gods of this world. I enlisted the services of other spirit helpers in attempting to fly through the far reaches of the Galaxy. Transported into a trance where the supernatural seemed natural,

---

* Accent in Jívaro is on the penultimate syllable unless otherwise indicated. A pair of dots over a vowel indicates that it is unvoiced.

I realized that anthropologists, including myself, had profoundly underestimated the importance of the drug in affecting native ideology. Therefore, in 1964 I returned to the Jívaro to give particular attention to the drug's use by the Jívaro shaman.

The use of the hallucinogenic *natemä* drink among the Jívaro makes it possible for almost anyone to achieve the trance state essential for the practice of shamanism. Given the presence of the drug and the felt need to contact the "real," or supernatural, world, it is not surprising that approximately one out of every four Jívaro men is a shaman. Women rarely become shamans but when they do they are thought to be particularly powerful because they are believed to possess special *tsentsak*—spirit helpers. Any adult, male or female, who desires to become such a practitioner, simply presents a gift to an already practicing shaman, who administers the *Banisteriopsis* drink and gives some of his own supernatural power—in the form *tsentsak*—to the apprentice. These spirit helpers, or "darts," are the main supernatural forces believed to cause illness and death in daily life. To the non-shaman they are normally invisible, and even shamans can perceive them only under the influence of *natemä*.

Shamans send these spirit helpers into the victims' bodies to make them ill or to kill them. At other times, they may suck spirits sent by enemy shamans from the bodies of tribesmen suffering from witchcraft-induced illness. The spirit helpers also form shields that protect their shaman masters from attacks. The following account presents the ideology of Jívaro witchcraft from the point of view of the Indians themselves.

To give the novice some *tsentsak*, the practicing shaman regurgitates what appears to be—to those who have taken *natemä* —a brilliant substance in which the spirit helpers are contained. He cuts part of it off with a machete and gives it to the novice to swallow. The recipient experiences pain upon taking it into his stomach and stays on his bed for ten days, drinking *natemä* every evening. The Jívaro believe they can keep magical darts in their stomachs indefinitely and regurgitate them at will. The shaman donating the *tsentsak* periodically blows and rubs all over the body of the novice, apparently to increase the power of the transfer.

A Jívaro shaman blows away the froth on the bubbling *natemä* brew to check its appearance

The novice must remain inactive and not engage in sexual intercourse for at least three months. If he fails in self-discipline, as some do, he will not become a successful shaman. At the end of the first month, a *tsentsak* emerges from his mouth. With this magical dart at his disposal, the new shaman experiences a tremendous desire to bewitch. If he casts his *tsentsak* to fulfill this desire, he will become a bewitching shaman. If, on the other

After the *natemä* has boiled down, and cooled it is ready to drink

hand, the novice can control his impulse and reswallow this first *tsentsak*, he will become a curing shaman.

If the shaman who gave the *tsentsak* to the new man was primarily a bewitcher, rather than a curer, the novice likewise will tend to become a bewitcher. This is because a bewitcher's magical darts have such a desire to kill that their new owner will be strongly inclined to adopt their attitude. One informant said that the urge to kill felt by bewitching shamans came to them with a strength and frequency similar to that of hunger.

Only if the novice shaman is able to abstain from sexual intercourse for five months, will he have the power to kill a man (if he is a bewitcher) or cure a victim (if he is a curer). A full year's abstinence is considered necessary to become a really effective bewitcher or curer.

During the period of sexual abstinence, the new shaman collects all kinds of insects, plants, and other objects, which he now has the power to convert into *tsentsak*. Almost any object, including living insects and worms, can become a *tsentsak* if it is small enough to be swallowed by a shaman. Different types of *tsentsak* are used to cause different kinds and degrees of illness. The greater the variety of these objects that a shaman has in his body, the greater is his ability.

According to Jívaro concepts, each *tsentsak* has a natural and supernatural aspect. The magical dart's natural aspect is that of an ordinary material object as seen without drinking the drug *natemä*. But the supernatural and "true" aspect of the *tsentsak* is revealed to the shaman by taking *natemä*. When he does this, the magical darts appear in new forms as demons and with new names. In their supernatural aspects, the *tsentsak* are not simply objects but spirit helpers in various forms, such as giant butterflies, jaguars, or monkeys, who actively assist the shaman in his tasks.

Bewitching is carried out against a specific, known individual and thus is almost always done to neighbors or, at the most, fellow tribesmen. Normally, as is the case with intratribal assassination, bewitching is done to avenge a particular offense committed against one's family or friends. Both bewitching and individual assassination contrast with the large-scale headhunting raids for which the Jívaro have become famous, and which were conducted against entire neighborhoods of enemy tribes.

To bewitch, the shaman takes *natemä* and secretly approaches the house of his victim. Just out of sight in the forest, he drinks green tobacco juice, enabling him to regurgitate a *tsentsak*, which he throws at his victim as he comes out of his house. If the *tsentsak* is strong enough and is thrown with sufficient force, it will pass all the way through the victim's body causing death within a period of a few days to several weeks. More often, however, the magical dart simply lodges in the victim's body. If the shaman, in his hiding place, fails to see the intended victim, he may instead bewitch any member of the intended victim's family who appears, usually a wife or child. When the shaman's mission is accomplished, he returns secretly to his own home.

One of the distinguishing characteristics of the bewitching process among the Jívaro is that, as far as I could learn, the victim is given no specific indication that someone is bewitching him. The bewitcher does not want his victim to be aware that he is being supernaturally attacked, lest he take protective measures by immediately procuring the services of a curing shaman. Nonetheless, shamans and laymen alike with whom I talked noted that illness invariably follows the bewitchment, although the degree of the illness can vary considerably.

A special kind of spirit helper, called a *pasuk*, can aid the bewitching shaman by remaining near the victim in the guise of an insect or animal of the forest after the bewitcher has left. This spirit helper has his own objects to shoot into the victim should a curing shaman succeed in sucking out the *tsentsak* sent earlier by the bewitcher who is the owner of the *pasuk*.

In addition, the bewitcher can enlist the aid of a *wakaní* ("soul," or "spirit") bird. Shamans have the power to call these birds and use them as spirit helpers in bewitching victims. The shaman blows on the *wakaní* birds and then sends them to the house of the victim to fly around and around the man, frightening him. This is believed to cause fever and insanity, with death resulting shortly thereafter.

After he returns home from bewitching, the shaman may send a *wakaní* bird to perch near the house of the victim. Then if a curing shaman sucks out the intruding object, the bewitching shaman sends the *wakaní* bird more *tsentsak* to throw from its beak into the victim. By continually resupplying the *wakaní* bird with new *tsentsak*, the sorcerer makes it impossible for the curer to rid his patient permanently of the magical darts.

While the *wakaní* birds are supernatural servants available to anyone who wishes to use them, the *pasuk*, chief among the spirit helpers, serves only a single shaman. Likewise a shaman possesses only one *pasuk*. The *pasuk*, being specialized for the service of bewitching, has a protective shield to guard it from counterattack by the curing shaman. The curing shaman, under the influence of *natemä*, sees the *pasuk* of the bewitcher in human form and size, but "covered with iron except for its eyes." The curing shaman can kill this *pasuk* only by shooting a *tsentsak* into its eyes, the sole vulnerable area in the *pasuk*'s armor. To the person who has not taken the hallucinogenic drink, the *pasuk* usually appears to be simply a tarantula.

Shamans also may kill or injure a person by using magical darts, *anamuk*, to create supernatural animals that attack a victim. If a shaman has a small, pointed armadillo bone *tsentsak*, he can shoot this into a river while the victim is crossing it on a balsa raft or in a canoe. Under the water, this bone manifests itself in its supernatural aspect as an anaconda, which rises up and overturns the craft, causing the victim to drown. The shaman can similarly use a tooth from a killed snake as a *tsentsak*, creating a poisonous serpent to bite his victim. In more or less the same manner, shamans can create jaguars and pumas to kill their victims.

About five years after receiving his *tsentsak*, a bewitching shaman undergoes a test to see if he still retains enough *tsentsak* power to continue to kill successfully. This test involves bewitching a tree. The shaman, under the influence of *natemä*, attempts to throw a *tsentsak* through the tree at the point where its two main branches join. If his strength and aim are adequate, the tree appears to split the moment the *tsentsak* is sent into it. The splitting, however, is invisible to an observer who is not under the influence of the hallucinogen. If the shaman fails, he knows that he is incapable of killing a human victim. This means that, as soon as possible, he must go to a strong shaman and purchase a new supply of *tsentsak*. Until he has the goods with which to pay for this new supply, he is in constant danger, in his proved weakened condition, of being seriously bewitched by other shamans. Therefore, each day, he drinks large quantities of *natemä*, tobacco juice, and the extract of yet another drug, *piripiri*. He also rests on his bed at home to conserve his strength, but tries to conceal his weakened condition from his enemies. When he purchases a new supply of *tsentsak*, he can safely cut down on his consumption of these other substances.

The degree of illness produced in a witchcraft victim is a function of both the force with which the *tsentsak* is shot into the body, and also of the character of the magical dart itself. If a *tsentsak* is shot all the way through the body of a victim, then "there is nothing for a curing shaman to suck out," and the patient dies. If the magical dart lodges within the body, however, it is theoretically possible to cure the victim by sucking. But in actual practice, the sucking is not always considered successful.

The work of the curing shaman is complementary to that of a bewitcher. When a curing shaman is called in to treat a patient, his first task is to see if the illness is due to witchcraft. The usual diagnosis and treatment begin with the curing shaman drinking *natemä*, tobacco juice, and *pirípiri* in the late afternoon and early evening. These drugs permit him to see into the body of the patient as though it were glass. If the illness is due to sorcery, the curing shaman will see the intruding object within the patient's body clearly enough to determine whether or not he can cure the sickness.

A shaman sucks magical darts from a patient's body only at night, and in a dark area of the house, for it is only in the dark that he can perceive the drug-induced visions that are the supernatural reality. With the setting of the sun, he alerts his *tsentsak* by whistling the tune of the curing song; after about a quarter of an hour, he starts singing. When he is ready to suck, the shaman regurgitates two *tsentsak* into the sides of his throat and mouth. These must be identical to the one he has seen in the patient's body. He holds one of these in the front of the mouth and the other in the rear. They are expected to catch the supernatural aspect of the magical dart that the shaman sucks out of the patient's body. The *tsentsak* nearest the shaman's lips is supposed to incorporate the sucked-out *tsentsak* essence within itself. If, however, this supernatural essence should get past it, the second magical dart in the mouth blocks the throat so that the intruder cannot enter the interior of the shaman's body. If the curer's two *tsentsak* were to fail to catch the supernatural essence of the *tsentsak*, it would pass down into the shaman's stomach and kill him. Trapped thus within the mouth, this essence is shortly caught by, and incorporated into, the material substance of one of the curing shaman's *tsentsak*. He then "vomits" out this object and displays it to the patient and his family saying, "Now I have sucked it out. Here it is."

The non-shamans think that the material object itself is what has been sucked out, and the shaman does not disillusion them. At the same time, he is not lying, because he knows that the only important thing about a *tsentsak* is its supernatural aspect, or essence, which he sincerely believes he has removed from the patient's body. To explain to the layman that he already had these objects in his mouth would serve no fruitful purpose and would prevent him from displaying such an object as proof that he had effected the cure. Without incontrovertible evidence, he would not be able to convince the patient and his family that he had effected the cure and must be paid.

The ability of the shaman to suck depends largely upon the quantity and strength of his own *tsentsak*, of which he may have hundreds. His magical darts assume their supernatural aspect as spirit helpers when he is under the influence of *natemä*, and he sees them as a variety of zoomorphic forms hovering over him, perching on his shoulders, and sticking out of his skin. He sees them helping to suck the patient's body. He must drink tobacco juice every few hours to "keep them fed" so that they will not leave him.

The curing shaman must also deal with any *pasuk* that may be in the patient's vicinity for the purpose of casting more darts. He drinks additional amounts of *natemä* in order to see them and engages in *tsentsak* duels with them if they are present. While the *pasuk* is enclosed in iron armor, the shaman himself has his own armor composed of his many *tsentsak*. As long as he is under the influence of *natemä*, these magical darts cover his body as a protective shield, and are on the lookout for any enemy *tsentsak* headed toward their master. When these *tsentsak* see such a missile coming, they immediately close up together at the point where the enemy dart is attempting to penetrate, and thereby repel it.

If the curer finds *tsentsak* entering the body of his patient after he has killed the *pasuk*, he suspects the presence of a *wakani* bird. He drinks *maikua* (*Datura arborea* or *suaveolens*), a hallucinogen even more powerful than *natemä*, as well as tobacco juice, and silently sneaks into the forest to kill the bird with *tsentsak*. When he succeeds, the curer returns to the patient's home, blows all over the house to get rid of the "atmosphere" created by the numerous *tsentsak* sent by the bird, and completes his sucking of the patient. Even after all the *tsentsak* are extracted, the shaman may remain another night at the house to suck out any "dirtiness" (*pahuri*) still inside. In the cures which I have witnessed, this sucking is a most noisy process, accompanied by deep, but dry, vomiting.

After sucking out a *tsentsak*, the shaman puts it into a little container. He does not swallow it because it is not his own magical dart and would therefore kill him. Later, he throws the *tsentsak* into the air, and it flies back to the shaman who sent it originally into the patient. *Tsentsak* also fly back to a shaman at the death of a former apprentice who had originally received them from him. Besides receiving "old" magical darts unexpectedly in this manner, the shaman may have *tsentsak* thrown at him by a bewitcher. Accordingly, shamans constantly drink tobacco juice at all hours of the day and night. Although the tobacco juice is not truly hallucinogenic, it produces a narcotized state, which is believed necessary to keep one's *tsentsak* ready to repel any other magical darts. A shaman does not even dare go for a walk without taking along the green tobacco leaves with which he prepares the juice that keeps his spirit helpers alert. Less frequently, but regularly, he must drink *natemä* for the same purpose and to keep in touch with the supernatural reality.

While curing under the influence of *natemä*, the curing shaman "sees" the shaman who bewitched his patient. Generally, he can recognize the person, unless it is a shaman who lives far away or in another tribe. The patient's family knows this, and demands to be told the identity of the bewitcher, particularly if the sick person dies. At one curing session I attended, the shaman could not identify the person he had seen in his vision. The brother of the dead man then accused the shaman himself of being responsible. Under such pressure, there is a strong tendency for the curing shaman to attribute each case to a particular bewitcher.

Shamans gradually become weak and must purchase *tsentsak* again and again. Curers tend to become weak in power, especially after curing a patient bewitched by a shaman who has recently received a new supply of magical darts. Thus, the most powerful shamans are those who can repeatedly purchase new supplies of *tsentsak* from other shamans.

Shamans can take back *tsentsak* from others to whom they have previously given them. To accomplish this, the shaman drinks *natemä*, and, using his *tsentsak*, creates a "bridge" in the form of a rainbow between himself and the other shaman. Then he shoots a *tsentsak* along this rainbow. This strikes the ground beside the other shaman with an explosion and flash likened to a lightning bolt. The purpose of this is to surprise the other shaman so that he temporarily forgets to maintain his guard over his magical darts, thus permitting the first shaman to suck them back along the rainbow. A shaman who has had his *tsentsak* taken away in this manner will discover that "nothing happens" when he drinks *natemä*. The sudden loss of his *tsentsak* will tend to make him ill, but ordinarily the illness is not fatal unless a bewitcher shoots a magical dart into him while he is in this weakened condition. If he has not become disillusioned by his experience, he can again purchase *tsentsak* from some other shaman and resume his calling. Fortunately for anthropology some of these men have chosen to give up shamanism and therefore can be persuaded to reveal their knowledge, no longer having a vested interest in the profession. This divulgence, however, does not serve as a significant threat to practitioners, for words alone can never adequately convey the realities of shamanism. These can only be approached with the aid of *natemä*, the chemical door to the otherwise invisible world of the Jívaro shaman.

REFERENCES

Agurell, S., B. Holmstedt and J. E. Lindgren
    1968   Alkaloid Content of Banisteriopsis Rusbyana. *American Journal of Pharmacy* 140: 148–51.

Der Marderosian, Ara
  1967   Hallucinogenic Indole Compounds from Higher Plants.
          Lloydia 30: 23–38.
Friedberg, Claudine
  1965   Des Banisteriopsis utilisés comme drogue en Amérique du
          Sud. *Journal d'Agriculture Tropicale et de Botanique Ap-
          pliquée* 12: 9–12.
Harner, Michael J.
  1972   *The Jívaro: People of the Sacred Waterfalls.* New York:
          Doubleday/Natural History Press.
Poisson, J.
  1965   Note sur le "Natem," boisson toxique péruvienne et ses
          alcaloïdes. *Annales Pharmaceutiques Françaises* 23: 241–44.

3

Visions and Cures Among
the Sharanahua

Janet Siskind

The shamans of the Sharanahua Indians of eastern Peru have learned to enter the dream world of their patients through the medium of the hallucinogenic drug *ayahuasca*. Patient and shaman communicate within a symbolic system validated by myth and belief and structured by the curing songs handed down from shaman to shaman.[1]

In *The Teachings of Don Juan*, Castaneda (1968) presents a description and analysis of his apprenticeship to a Yaqui shaman. Through Don Juan's careful instruction in the powers and use of several hallucinogenic plants, Castaneda begins to find his way in the "non-ordinary reality" of visions. Perhaps under no other conditions is it possible for an adult to so fully re-enter the enculturation situation, where experience is intense and chaotic and, with learning, slowly becomes structured and communicable.

JANET SISKIND, PH.D., is an Assistant Professor of Anthropology at Rutgers—The State University (Newark, New Jersey). She specializes in the culture of the Sharanahua of eastern Peru, neighbors of the Cashinahua, to whom she has made three trips.

1. The fieldwork on which the article is based is part of a research project on drugs, sponsored and supported by the Instituto de Psiquiatria Social, of the Universidad Nacional Mayor de San Marcos and supported by Foundations Fund for Research in Psychiatry. It was a continuation of my ethnographic work among the Sharanahua, begun in 1966–67.

Castaneda's study takes us into the process by which the apprentice shaman, like a child differentiating phonemes from noise,
learns to choose among illusory or idiosyncratic visions, the true,
correct, culturally approved images. This process, which Castaneda
describes as "consensual validation," has taught us our roles, our
taboos, our perceptions, and our fears, as well as our languages.
He shows us that the organization of drug-induced visual experience is structured through learning. I hope to show that the organization of hallucinatory experience among the Sharanahua is structured as a form of communication between patient and shaman,
and that these communications are related to the consensually
validated organization of their social world.

Along the banks of the Upper Purús River, where the eastern
border of Peru juts abruptly into Brazil, are a number of Indian
groups who have migrated during the last thirty years from the
tributaries of the Taruacá River. All but one of these groups
speaks a Panoan language and, despite dialectical variations, they
are able to understand one another.

There is evidence that names such as "Sharanahua," "good
people," were once applied to moieties. Today these names, which
are inherited patrilineally, do not refer to any cohesive group.
The important social units are small, exogamous descent groups
made up of close kin. Settlements consist of members of two or
more of these descent groups linked by marriage.

Matrilocality is followed rather strictly, which leads to a male
preference for village endogamy and cross-cousin marriage. This
preference reflects the old days of warfare, when it was dangerous
to be a stranger without kin even in another Sharanahua village.
There is still a feeling of discomfort at living in a village where
one has no kin. A scarcity of women in one village, however, often
forces men to search for wives in another. The village of Marcos,
where field-work was carried out, consists mainly of Sharanahua,
but also includes men of other groups who have married into
Sharanahua households and a few women, mostly second wives,
who were orphaned and are living with their husband's people.

The Sharanahua distinguish a number of different categories of
people along a close-distant dimension. *Unwu yura*, "my kin" is
the closest. *Doku kaifo*, "our people," are those one may trust or,

more accurately, people one does not derogate and does not automatically distrust. Chosinahua and Marinahua are included with Sharanahua in this category. The rest of the world consists of *yura wutsa*, "other people," a term of derogation for other Indians, and *dawa*, Peruvians, a dangerous and admired group.

Thirty years ago, when the Sharanahua and neighboring groups entered the Upper Purús region, there were no other Indians along the river. The rubber boom had come and gone, enslaving and eliminating the Indians whom Chandless (1866) had seen when he explored the river in the 1860's. There were a few Peruvians and Brazilians with whom the Sharanahua began to trade. Trading skins for trade goods is becoming an important part of Sharanahua life. Clothing, mosquito nets, machetes, shotguns, metal pots, and several other items are regarded as necessities. The common system of buying on credit and payment in goods exists here as throughout the tropical forest. Indians are cheated here as elsewhere, but there are no strong patróns in this area.

This corner of the tropical forest is extremely isolated and sparsely populated, so that much remains of an indigenous way of life. Subsistence rests on slash and burn agriculture, which produces good crops of plantains, bananas, sweet manioc, maize, and peanuts. Game is abundant, and hunting is a major focus of time and thought. Fishing is beginning to increase in importance, and gathering adds further variety to the diet.

The Sharanahua were badly hit by contact with foreign diseases ten to twenty years ago, and genealogies indicate the tremendous losses they have suffered. Today they are on the upswing, with births far outnumbering deaths. In this region Indian villages are free of malaria and tuberculosis. There are no endemic diseases and—with the exception of a mumps epidemic a few years ago which claimed no mortalities—no epidemic diseases. The most common health problems are amoebae and intestinal worms, bacterial and viral dysenteries, and respiratory infections.

The Sharanahua utilize a variety of methods to cure the sick. Minor wounds and ailments are generally cared for by the application of herbs and leaves. Stomach pains and diarrheas are often handled by changing the diet. When the illness appears more serious, one of the men of the household will blow smoke over the patient's body, rubbing the ailment out. When more specialized knowledge is needed, one of the older men, Basta, is consulted. He is not a shaman but he is expert at the selection and preparation of herbal remedies, handling a range of ailments from severe toothache to serious wounds. A practical people, the Sharanahua accept penicillin eagerly, noting its often remarkable results and are not discouraged by its limitations. The introduction of antibiotics by missionaries has lessened the shaman's work load, but the Sharanahua's faith and dependence upon the shamans are undiminished.

Sharanahua shamans take part in everyday life; they are part-time specialists. They are respected and feared since they are able to kill as well as cure. Three of the twenty-five men at the village of Marcos are shamans: Casha, Baido, and Ndaishiwaka. I worked intensively with Ndaishiwaka, going over the cases he had treated within the past few years and his procedures in each case. We discussed twenty-seven cases.

Sharanahua shamans rarely use the common South American technique of sucking out a magically harmful object, even though the Culina, a neighboring group of Arawak-speakers, are feared for their ability to kill or cause illness by throwing *dori*, a magical substance, into the bodies of their victims. The Sharanahua seek the cause of illness in an *ayahuasca* vision; and the shaman cures by singing. He can cure all illnesses except those caused by a large quantity of *dori*. These cases are sometimes sent to the Culina village for cure. All deaths, therefore, are blamed on the Culina, since it is said that any other illness can be cured by the singing of the Sharanahua shamans.

The songs are about almost every part of the environment. There is, for example, a song about each of the twelve varieties of plantains that the Sharanahua know. There are songs about each animal, and songs about recently encountered objects, such as motor boats, airplanes, and radios. These songs are sung in an esoteric form of the language, difficult to understand, and filled with metaphors. Each symptom and illness has many songs; some are considered stronger than others. After many months of writing down these songs I was told by my informant that they can be used to induce illness as well as cure. He claimed to have killed two Culina by singing them to death.

The curing songs and the visions of *ayahuasca* are learned by an apprentice shaman during a year or more of intensive training. For the Sharanahua, singing is closely bound to *ayahuasca*. Men chant when they take it, and they claim that without singing only visions of snakes appear. Other visions come when the songs call them. Like most Sharanahua men, the shaman Ndaishiwaka had taken *ayahuasca* many times and had overcome his terror of the first frightening hallucinations of snakes before he decided to become a shaman. He knew the song of the spirit of *ayahuasca* that everyone knows. He was about eighteen years old when a venomous snake bit him and he was going to die. Two shamans, Forako, his father's brother, and Casha, cured him, and he desired to become a shaman. During the period of his apprenticeship, Ndaishiwaka maintained a strict diet and celibacy. A snake's tongue was rubbed over him, and he ate the heart of a boa constrictor. Forako and Casha taught him all the curing songs and, as he continued to take *ayahuasca*, he gradually began to see more elaborate visions. Finally he was able to see the man of *ayahuasca* and the spirits of *ayahuasca* who aid the shamans. He returned to normal life and the practice of shamanism.

The choice of songs that the shaman sings is based on two factors: the symptoms and the dream of the patient. These are not independent data. The patient usually reports dream images that overlap or coincide with the shamans' categories of songs and symptoms. The shaman also selects from the patient's reported dream those images that fit his song classification. One of the striking things about the dreams of his patients, described to me by the shaman, was their simplicity. One or perhaps two images are mentioned. In the cases described below, the patient dreams of a peccary, or the sun, or of climbing up a high bank on the river. The dreams are not reported as stories or interactions, yet from dreams collected outside of the curing situation I know that the more usual pattern of Sharanahua dreams is of people and sequential events.

Most of the symbols described in these dreams and the *ayahuasca* visions of the shaman echo myths and stories. Animals appear frequently, and the changeability of men into animals and animals into men is a common theme. According to Sharanahua myth all animals were originally human. The Sharanahua say, *doku kuscura,* "our type."

It is not the type of illness that dictates the necessity of calling the shaman, but rather its intensity or severity. This is marked by the subjective experience of the patient which leads him to refuse food. This behavior is translated by his kin to signify *da pai,* that he wants to die. It is a signal that involves the entire circle of kin. Women enter the patient's mosquito net, hold him in their arms, while all weep and chant, "My child is dying, my child is dying." One of the men of the kin group will then go to call a shaman.

The shaman asks the sick man about his symptoms and his dreams. Either the shaman or a close male relative of the patient prepares and cooks the leaves of *chacruna* and the liana of *aya-huasca* to concoct a hallucinogenic brew. (Sometimes, when *ayahuasca* is not easily available, shamans begin curing without taking it, and procure it the next day if the patient is still sick.) Early in the evening the shaman and most of the other men begin to drink the cooled liquid. The men chant; the shaman sings a curing song; and slowly a vision appears before his eyes of the image from the sick man's dream. The shaman speaks of his vision as he experiences it.[2] A few of his cases are described below.

Ndaishiwaka's sister-in-law, Tomuha, was vomiting; her liver hurt, and she strongly wanted to die. Her father-in-law went to bring Ndaishiwaka (he was working away from the village at the time). The next morning he arrived at the village. He asked Tomuha what she had dreamed, and she described seeing a high bank of the river. In her dreams she climbed up and sat there alone. Then the shaman sang about a high bank on the river. Tomuha was slightly better the next day but still very ill, so he went to get *ayahuasca,* cooked it, and drank it that night. He saw the high bank and Tomuha sitting alone. A Culina is coming

2. Although *ayahuasca* visions are quite literally entrancing, it is possible to talk about them as they occur and to remember them clearly long afterwards.

near her and he says, "You will die, Tomuha," and throws a magical substance into her so that she vomits and cries out. "But I am there," says the shaman, "and I am shaking my spear, and the Culina is frightened and runs away. And you will not die, Tomuha." Then the shaman sang about *dori*, the magical substance. He saw Tomuha coming up the river, alone in a canoe. She was cured.

Tomuha is about thirty years old and married to the shaman's youngest brother. Her father was a Yaminahua, her mother a Culina who subsequently married a Culina. Many of her relatives, including her first child, had been killed by Culina sorcery.

Yopira, a woman of about thirty, is the second wife of Baido, another shaman. Her stomach had ached for days, and she slept and slept. Baido and Casha (the third shaman) had tried to cure her without success. Baido called Ndaishiwaka, and he came. The three shamans took *ayahuasca*, but Baido and Casha could not cure her. Yopira had dreamed of a capybara, and when Ndaishiwaka took *ayahuasca* he saw the capybara going around Yopira, clawing her back, and eating her. Ndaishiwaka told Yopira to make a big fire to burn the capybara, and the capybara died. He told Yopira and Baido to eat the capybara, which they did, even though they were unable to see it. Then Ndaishiwaka saw a ghost, a man who looked like a monkey, taking *ayahuasca*. Yopira was cured. During this cure, Ndaishiwaka sang for two days, taking *ayahuasca* both nights. In addition to the capybara, which he felt was the significant vision and song, he had also seen and sung of the land turtle and a particular type of snake.

Chicolopez, a man of about fifty-five, is the shaman's "other father," or father's brother. Ndaishiwaka was called to the village where Chicolopez was living. He had a bad headache and shook all over. The Dominican padre had given him pills and injections of penicillin, but Chicolopez was still very sick. Chicolopez had dreamed of a huge monkey, like a howler monkey but very large. A male with painted designs on its forehead, white hands, and white feet. Ndaishiwaka took *ayahuasca* and sang of the howler monkey, then he saw it, a huge one, it was eating fruit in the trees. It grabbed Chicolopez, but the shaman told it to leave him alone, and it ran away. The next night the shaman saw a different kind of monkey. It was black and white, and it was eating people. There were lots of people and lots of monkeys eating them. They wanted to eat Chicolopez. A huge one was coming; the shaman took a bow and arrow and hit them all. They yelled and ran away in all directions. The shaman told Chicolopez, "You dreamed of these monkeys, now I see them. I hit them with my bow and they are running away." The third night Chicolopez dreamed of a peccary. In his subsequent hallucination, the shaman saw a huge peccary coming toward Chicolopez, biting him. Ndaishiwaka shot the peccary with his shotgun. It did not die, but it ran away. Then Chicolopez began to eat a little. His shaking lessened. On the fourth night Ndaishiwaka sang about *mama*, the traditional unfermented corn drink. The next morning he gave some to Chicolopez. He was well.

Though it is usual to have more than one shaman take part in a cure, my informant always claimed the credit for success. When the shaman's father, Baiyakondi, was vomiting, Ndaishiwaka sang of watermelons and had a vision of lots of watermelons on the beach. His father was eating them, and he told him to stop. In the vision Baiyakondi stops and is cured. The other shaman, Baido, saw a huge fish. The fish was eating Baiyakondi, so Baido sang about the fish. The fish went away, but Baiyakondi was not cured. Unfortunately I have no record of the dream in this case, but it seems likely that the elements in the dream were differently used by the two shamans. It also appears likely that had my informant been Baido, the story might be different.

In several cases, elements of Peruvian culture appear. Ruatay, a girl of about eleven, was sick while I was working in the village. For a week she had run high fevers, which tended to drop in the mornings. She had what appeared to be grippe and a bad cough. I was unsuccessful in treating her with a broad-spectrum antibiotic. It was probably a severe viral infection.

Ruatay had dreamed of an airplane and of the sun's hurting her. (It is usual to complain of the "sun hurting" if one must be exposed to it for several hours in the middle of the day.) Ndaishiwaka sang of the plane and he saw Ruatay flying on it.

As he continued to sing the plane vanished, and Ruatay was cured.

One of the shaman's younger brothers, Tohuikai, about thirty-five years of age, had been sick with grippe for six days (grippe is considered to be a Peruvian disease). He had a high fever and was coughing blood. Ndaishiwaka called Felisario (a famous shaman who used to live in the same village) and they took *ayahuasca*. I do not have a record of the dream. Ndaishiwaka saw an accordian grabbing Tohuikai around the chest. He sang of the accordian, and it went away. Felisario saw a harmonica, which also went away as he continued to sing, and Tohuikai was a little better. Then Ndaishiwaka saw a bead necklace, beads of white, red, and black (necklaces are made by the Sharanahua from beads purchased from Peruvian traders) which was strangling Tohuikai. He sang about the necklace; it went away and Tohuikai got better.

The Peruvian images underline a piece of Sharanahua belief: strangers are dangerous. Direct malice, however, in the form of deliberate sorcery is assigned only to the Culina. The Culina appear to be a scapegoat for the general suspicion of *yura wutsa*, "other people." The suspicion of Culina sorcery is raised particularly when anyone becomes sick who has had any contact with them, as in the case cited above of Tomuha who is herself part Culina. Also, when her husband, Iconahua, was very sick, it was Culina sorcery that was the cause. The shaman sang for four days and nights to cure him. The Culina had sorcerized him because he had taken Tomuha from their village.

When the patient starts to improve, the shaman retires to his own house, drinks a small amount of *ayahuasca* from a special small clay pot, and then sings into the pot, which produces a strange vibrating sound in the singing. The next morning the shaman offers his patient a drink of *mama* from this pot. Usually a patient takes nothing but corn drink and boiled banana drink for a day. Then he eats fish, and when fully recovered returns to his normal diet.

The shaman is an expert at the art of intense direct communication. The case of Tomuha was described to me with particular care. It is difficult for me to convey in words the clarity with which the shaman describes his vision and the emotional impact, emphasized dramatically by touch, of his reassurance, "You will not die, Tomuha." I heard only the report of a vision that had occurred over a year previously. The impact would be more intense during an actual cure, when a patient listens to the shaman describe a vision constructed of symbols from the patient's dream.

The sharing of symbols between at least two people is the basis for any communication system. Dream and vision symbolism among the Sharanahua does not involve a one-to-one relationship of meaning and symbol, but neither is there complete free rein for idiosyncratic dreaming or hallucinating. Both shaman and patient are bound by the limits of the curing song classification of symbol and symptoms. A patient who dreamed of a bead necklace after cutting his foot would not be communicating since he would have chosen a symbol that is not appropriate for his symptoms. A shaman who selected the image of a land turtle from the dream of a patient suffering from headache and fever would not be talking the patient's language. Yet there is sufficient overlap and redundance of symbols, especially with regard to the most common serious ailments: bloody diarrhea, stomach ache, and grippe with high fever, for individual feelings to be expressed by the patient and picked up by the shaman.[3]

The training of a shaman is a process in which he learns to express his perceptions in the language of song and vision. Although the curing trances are supposedly to discover the causes of an illness, it seems that the shaman uses them to tune in on his feeling about the patient. Long experience and shamanistic training combine to give the shaman a certain amount of control of his visions, and the patient's dream provides "suggestion" to the receptive, hallucinating shaman. The shaman's rapport with his patient is expressed by the description of the *ayahuasca* vision, which restates the patient's dream. What then is the communication in this interaction?

3. Future research may clarify who, and to what degree, the shaman or the patient, makes the selection of symbols. My informant reported each dream as if the patient only mentioned one or two images, and, unfortunately, it did not occur to me to investigate this more fully while I was in the field.

Sharanahua shamans, like shamans everywhere, are often successful in their cures. But, as Jerome Frank (1961) has shown, almost any method of curing that is not actually detrimental to health relieves symptoms most of the time if the patient believes in it. The question raised is not how this system works to effect a cure, but rather what kind of message is communicated between patient and shaman. The answer appears in the context in which the shaman is called. A Sharanahua shows that "he wants to die," and his circle of kin chant, "My child is dying." The statement is not that death is imminent. (I have heard these chants over and over again, and no one has died during the three years I have been in contact with the Sharanahua.) It represents some experience of separation from the kin group. The communication between the shaman and his patient is a bridge across which the patient returns.

If a patient's dream expresses some feeling of alienation the shaman's choice of symbol and vision is based on his perception of how to diminish the patient's alienation from his kin group. The animal images which are of "our type" may represent some view of the difficult nature of dealing with the people in one's social world. Images of "other people," or manufactured objects may express curiosity about the outside world, leading away from the closed circle of kin. The shaman enters the dream, controls the animal-like creatures, and rescues his patient from the deadly interaction with strangers.

This language of vision and dream has been learned within the constructs of Sharanahua society, in which the kin group is the crucial unit. The reality of Sharanahua life, consensually validated like the shaman's *ayahuasca* visions, is that life is possible only within the circle of kin.

REFERENCES

Castaneda, Carlos
    1968 *The Teachings of Don Juan.* Berkeley and Los Angeles, University of California Press.

Chandless, W.
  1866 Ascent of the River Purús. *Journal of the Royal Geographic Society* 24:86–118.
Frank, Jerome
  1961 *Persuasion and Healing*. Baltimore, The Johns Hopkins Press.

4

Shamanism and Priesthood in the Light of the Campa Ayahuasca Ceremony

Gerald Weiss

We have come to recognize two main types of religious practitioners, the shaman and the priest. The shaman is found typically in tribal cultures, the priest in state formations and so, presumably, later in appearance, although some overlap between the two may occur. The picture we derive from the literature on this subject presents a sharp contrast between shaman and priest: we conceive of them as qualitatively different. We think of a shaman as obtaining his powers primarily from direct contact with spirits, of a priest as one who earns his credentials primarily through special training (Lowie, 1954:179). We think of a shaman as an independent practitioner operating on a part-time basis, of a priest as a member of an organization consisting of full-time specialists (Beals and Hoijer, 1965:585–86; Hoebel, 1966:482; Jacobs, 1964: 281). We see a shaman as one who focuses his professional skills on individuals, particularly for purposes of curing, a priest as one who leads group activities of a ceremonial nature (Beals and Hoijer, 1965:586; Norbeck, 1961:103). We see the activity of a

GERALD WEISS, PH.D., is Associate Professor of Anthropology at Florida Atlantic University, Boca Raton, Florida. He conducted field research between 1960 and 1964 among the Campa of the eastern Peruvian rain forest. An earlier version of this paper was read in the Hallucinogens and Shamanism symposium at the annual meeting of the American Anthropological Association in Seattle in 1968.

shaman as characterized by possession, trance, and frenzy, while we see a priest conducting routine propitiatory acts of adoration, prayer, and offerings (Casanowicz, 1925; Lowie, 1940:310–11; Norbeck, 1961:103–5; Shirokogoroff, 1923; Wissler, 1938:201–6).

Broadly speaking, it is in such terms that the distinction between shaman and priest is made. One difficulty which has been overlooked, however, is that in these terms there is no point of contact between the two: they are simply two different kinds of religious practitioner, as different from and unrelated to one another as carpenters and potters among artisans. As a consequence, we are faced with the following question: where did the priest, as the later form, come from? Did he spring up out of nowhere as an independent development to challenge the shaman, or is there not some point of contact, some area of overlap that would allow us to entertain the possibility that priests developed historically out of shamans?

The notion that priests are the offspring of shamans has been argued by some writers. Sternberg (1925:502) suggests a development from shaman to priest with a concomitant shift from possession to solicitation, from spirit to god, and from hut to temple. Chapple and Coon (1942:407–12), while using "shaman" and "priest" interchangeably in referring to religious practitioners, nevertheless postulate that an original generalized practitioner came in time to be specialized along a number of different lines, one of these being that of a specialist in ritual. If we entertain this possibility, however, as I propose to do here, there remains the question of how the shift might have come about, especially since the archetypal shaman and priest are commonly presented as qualitatively different in their manner of conducting professional activities.

In keeping with Chapple and Coon's developmental scheme, let us take "shaman" to mean a generalized or undifferentiated religious practitioner, one who combines general contact with the supernatural realm and application of this contact, particularly in curing. Such a practitioner is generally associated with those characteristics that have been mentioned as setting him apart qualitatively from the priest. Let us take "priest" to mean a religious practitioner specializing in ritual, and further typified by those

The Campa shaman Porekavánti

distinctive characteristics already mentioned for him. In the
terms, a priest may be distinguished from a generalized prac
tioner or shaman, and from other specialized practitioners, such
the diviner, the prophet, and the specialized curer.

It is also important to establish that, where he makes his a
pearance, the shaman engages not only in individual curing, b
also in a particular form of group ceremony or ritual which
recognize as a shamanistic performance or séance. This shama
istic ritual/typically (or archetypically) incorporates such elemen
as spirit-possession, soul-flight, ventriloquism, and movement
objects, all effected by the shaman, whose behavior combin
frenzy and trance, while the assembled laymen remain passi
observers. A shamanistic performance in these particulars diffe
from a typical priestly ritual, which might be described as form
worship since it involves a reverent formalism that excluc
frenzy, and acts of propitiation or adoration that exclude v

tuosity. In these terms, it is difficult to see in a priest a specialized shaman, for a priest's professional activities appear to fall entirely outside the range of shamanistic behavior.

With these considerations in mind, let us inspect the form of the shamanistic performance I observed among the Campa of eastern Peru. This ceremony, utilizing the hallucinogenic drug *ayahuasca (Banisteriopsis)*, would appear to be unusual in certain respects, and may exemplify the kind of transitional situation that would permit the transformation of shaman into priest.

The leader of this ceremony among the Campa is a religious practitioner identifiable without question as a shaman. He is a man who has passed through a period of apprenticeship but who, during that period and ever after, obtains, maintains, and increases his recognized special powers solely by the continual and heroic consumption of drugs: primarily tobacco, particularly in the form of a concentrated syrup, and *ayahuasca*. The importance of these substances is indicated by the word for shaman in the Campa language: *sheripiári*, which contains the Campa term for tobacco (*shéri*). Tobacco is not an hallucinogen, but in massive doses it is a powerful intoxicant. As such, it is credited as the general source of a Campa shaman's powers to see and communicate with the spirits and to cure or (rather) to diagnose illness. *Ayahuasca* is an hallucinogen which puts him directly into communication with the spirit world, as spirits visit him, or as his soul leaves his body to visit the abodes of the spirits and other distant places.

Campa shamans take *ayahuasca* frequently, often keeping a supply on hand for this purpose. But in addition, from time to time, by decision or request, they conduct a group ceremony involving *ayahuasca*, which we can refer to as the Campa *ayahuasca* ceremony. This ceremony is essentially a shamanistic séance, but of a somewhat distinctive kind.

The Campa *ayahuasca* ceremony begins at nightfall since the drug requires darkness to produce its visual effects. A quantity of the drug, in the form of a thick liquid, is prepared in advance and set aside for use in the ceremony. The drug itself is called *kamárampi* in the Campa language, from the verb root *-kamarank-*, which means "to vomit," reflecting its extremely bitter and some-times emetic qualities. It is prepared by boiling fragments of *ayahuasca* vine (also called *kamárampi*) which the Campa find growing wild and transplant to the vicinity of their settlements, combined with leaves from an uncultivated tree bearing the Campa name of *horóva* (*Psychotria viridis*).

At nightfall, those who are present convene, arranging them-selves sitting or lying on mats out in the open of the settlement clearing, or else under a house roof, the women separated from the men in the Campa fashion. The shaman is the center of at-tention, with the vessel containing the *kamárampi* by him. Using a small gourd bowl, he drinks a quantity of the liquid, then gives each of the other participants a drink—a procedure that will be repeated at intervals until the supply is consumed. About half an hour later, the drug begins to take effect, and the shaman begins to sing. He sings one song after another as long as he is under the influence of the drug, and the séance may last until dawn.

There is a distinctive quality to the singing of a Campa shaman under the influence of *kamárampi*, an eerie, distant quality of voice. His jaw may quiver, he may cause his clothing to vibrate. What is understood to be happening is that the good spirits have come to visit the group that has called them: they come in human form, festively attired; they sing and dance before the assembled mortals, but only the shaman perceives them clearly. It is further understood that when the shaman sings he is only repeating what he hears the spirits sing, he is merely singing along with them. At no time is he possessed by a spirit, since Campa culture does not include a belief in spirit-possession.

Even while the shaman is singing, his soul may go on a flight to some distant place, returning later. Some shamans move from the sight of the rest of the group during the ceremony and then pretend to disappear bodily on such a flight, only to return later. The soul-flight of the shaman is an optional concomitant in any case, and in its usual form is a personal experience that does not intrude upon the actual performance of the ceremony.

The songs mainly extol the excellence and bounty of the good spirits. One song marks the appearance of the hawk *Koákiti* in human form:

Tobacco, tobacco, pure tobacco
It comes from River's Beginning
Koákiti, the hawk, brings it to you
Its flowers are flying, tobacco
It comes to your [or our] aid, tobacco
Tobacco, tobacco, pure tobacco
Koákiti, the hawk, is its owner

The following lines are from a song marking the appearance of hummingbird spirits:

Hummingbirds, hummingbirds, they come running
Hummingbirds, hummingbirds, dark appearance
Hummingbirds, hummingbirds, all our brothers
Hummingbirds, hummingbirds, they all hover
Hummingbirds, hummingbirds, group without blemish

The entire atmosphere of the ceremony is one of decorum without frenzy, even though the shaman is in a drugged trance. The ceremony, following a definite if simple format, presents the appearance of a group of people reverently making contact with the good spirits under the leadership of a religious practitioner, even though it is true that they remain passively appreciative spectators of the shaman's virtuosity.

Thus, the Campa *kamárampi* ceremony is definitely a shamanistic performance. The spirits communicate through the shaman to the spectators, and the shaman puts on a show. Nevertheless, the particular way in which these objectives are accomplished embodies a certain ambiguity or ambivalence, because the very same acts are acts of worship as well, as the shaman, leader of the group, reverently makes contact with the good spirits and praises them in song. To this extent the ceremony takes on certain of the distinctive qualities of priestly ritual. The effect is that of an optical illusion (Necker illusion) to an observer preconditioned to recognize the difference between the two: the same behavior looks like a séance one moment and like worship the next.

That we have here a true and not merely an apparent ambivalence is suggested by a special local variation of the *kamárampi* ceremony in which the element of worship or adoration is more strongly pronounced. In one part of Campa territory that I visited, the ceremony proceeds as described, except that the men take turns singing so that the shaman remains the director of the ceremony but is no longer the only virtuoso. In addition, the men and the women separately and together dance and sing in praise of the good spirits. Here the arrow of communication is unambiguously from mortals to immortals rather than the reverse, and it is in the form of adoration. Some recent missionary influence may be suspected in this case, but we are definitely still operating within the framework of the basic Campa *kamárampi* ceremony, the main difference being that the element of worship has come to be accentuated and stripped of much of its ambiguity.

These, then, are the facts relevant to our problem. With respect to their interpretation, a number of alternative possibilities exist, none of which can be entirely ruled out. First, it remains possible that the points of similarity between the Campa shamanistic performance and true priestly ritual are only apparent and not real, or are not significant. Second, whatever their status, there is no certainty that from this kind of shamanistic performance true priestly ritual emerged as a matter of historical fact. Third, it is possible that Andean or missionary influence has infused the Campa shamanistic performance with the flavor of priestly ritual, given the proximity of Campa territory to the former Incan empire with its full-blown priesthood, and more than three centuries of European missionary activity among the Campa.

But there remains another possibility suggested by the Campa data, one which deserves some attention in thinking about the circumstances leading to the emergence of the priest. It is possible that the total range of variation of shamanistic phenomena unaffected by any already existing priesthood includes a rather special variant of the usual shamanistic ritual. This variant is not necessarily common, but its features are ambivalent in such a way that a slight shift in how the participants interpret what they are doing could transform an essentially shamanistic séance into a priestly ritual. If this is indeed the case, then we may have discovered the behavioral link between generalized shamans and specialized priests that could have permitted the transition from one to the other.

REFERENCES

Beals, Ralph L., and Harry Hoijer
  1965 *An Introduction to Anthropology*. 3d ed. New York: Mac-
        millan.
Casanowicz, I. M.
  1925 Shamanism of the Natives of Siberia. *Annual Report of the
        Smithsonian Institution*, 1924, pp. 415–34.
Chapple, Eliot D., and Carleton S. Coon
  1942 *Principles of Anthropology*. New York: Holt.
Hoebel, E. Adamson
  1966 *Anthropology: The Study of Man*. New York: McGraw-Hill.
Jacobs, Melville
  1964 *Pattern in Cultural Anthropology*. Homewood, Ill.: Dorsey.
Lowie, Robert H.
  1940 *An Introduction to Cultural Anthropology*. New York: Rine-
        hart.
  1954 *Indians of the Plains*. New York: McGraw-Hill.
Norbeck, Edward
  1961 *Religion in Primitive Society*. New York: Harper and Row.
Shirokogoroff, S. M.
  1923 General Theory of Shamanism among the Tungus. *Journal
        of the Royal Asiatic Society of Great Britain and Ireland*,
        North China Branch (Shanghai), 54:246–49.
Sternberg, Leo
  1925 Divine Election in Primitive Religion. *Proceedings of the
        21st International Congress of Americanists*, 1924, Pt. II
        (Göteborg), pp. 472–512.
Wissler, Clark
  1938 *The American Indian: An Introduction to the Anthropology
        of the New World*. 3d ed. New York: Oxford University
        Press.

II

In Cultures Undergoing Westernization

THE SPREAD of Western society, economy, and culture throughout the world during the past few centuries has usually included the introduction of Christian beliefs into native contexts. The resulting combination of non-Western and Western religious ideologies has included syncretisms which involve the use of traditional hallucinogens invoked in the name of supernatural figures in the Christian pantheon.

Probably the most famous combination of hallucinogenic drug use and Christianity is the Native American Church, whose practitioners are American Indians in the United States who have largely adopted the mescaline-containing peyote since the latter part of the nineteenth century, and still use it, believing that with its aid they can both "talk" with Jesus and cure illness.

Elsewhere, we find a more ancient use of native hallucinogens combined with an overlay of Christian elements, as among the Indian peasants and mestizos (persons of mixed Indian and European ancestry and culture) in portions of Mexico and Peru. In such cases, rites are conducted primarily for the purpose of supernatural curing along the lines of ancient shamanism. While such practitioners are usually frowned upon by local ecclesiastical authorities, and may even be referred to by the latter as "witches," the general populace often employs their services heavily and views them as "curers" (*curanderos*), who through their ability to contact and control supernatural forces are able to provide services not available from the established Church or even from the medical profession, at least at prices the peasant or slum dweller can afford.

Since the peyote cult is relatively well known (e.g. La Barre, 1969; Slotkin, 1956), the only paper in the present volume dealing with peyote concerns the unusual case of its temporary adoption and subsequent rejection among the Apaches of the Mescalero Indian Reservation in New Mexico. In this article, Boyer, Boyer, and Basehart suggest that Mescalero socialization procedures develop adults whose hostilities are repressed only with difficulty. Boyer *et al*. propose that the physio-psychological effects of peyote made it impossible for many individuals to repress their hostilities, with the result that peyote meetings gave rise to disruption, bloodshed, and feuds. Finally, peyote became defined as an evil substance and general use of peyote by the populace was abandoned. The few individuals who still employ it are shamans and pseudo-shamans who are believed by the Mescalero to be using it for malevolent ends in witchcraft. The Mescalero case contrasts with the usual picture of amiable, harmonious group sessions of peyote use in other North American tribes and with the similarly harmonious communal use of *ayahuasca* among the Cashinahua, Sharanahua, and Campa of the Peruvian Amazon. The paper on the Mescalero Reservation Apaches serves to illustrate the importance of personality and culture in affecting the impact of the hallucinogenic drug experience and of the experience itself in triggering social behavior already latently possible. As in the case of the Jívaro of the Ecuadorian Amazon, hallucinogen use among the Mescalero is identified with individualistic and often hostile supernatural activity.

The importance of culture in affecting the role and impact of hallucinogen use is also stressed by Dobkin de Rios in her contribution on shamanistic curing in the eastern Peruvian city of Iquitos. Here she found slum-dwellers of mixed Indian-white ancestry ascribing illness to supernatural causation when modern Western medicine failed to provide a cure. Such ascription, based on both native American and European beliefs concerning witchcraft as a source of illness, leads the slum-dwellers to seek the services of an *ayahuasquero*, a mestizo shaman using *ayahuasca*, to cure the illness. This inclination to employ an *ayahuasquero* is reinforced by the comparatively high cost of formal medical consultation.

The *ayahuasquero* and his patients partake of the hallucinogenic drink together, the curer using the trance state to determine the cause of each patient's illness. The sickness is typically ascribed to a specific bewitcher in each case, a practice which Dobkin de Rios sees as a therapeutically effective means of transforming the generalized and incapacitating anxiety of the slum-dwellers "into solid fear that is placed squarely on the shoulders of some evildoer." The hallucinations of the group session and the guidance provided by the shaman are viewed as agents which reinforce the patient's belief in the reality of the shaman's power and information. Dobkin de Rios contrasts the role of *ayahuasca* in this situation with the use of related drugs in Western psychotherapy, where their role is primarily "to open areas of repressed and painful memories."

The *ayahuasqueros* in some cases go beyond simply identifying the miscreant responsible for the illness, to punishing them, maintaining "that while intoxicated by the drug, they can leave their bodies and inflict harm and even incurable disease upon their clients' enemies." In this, their beliefs resemble those reported for traditional European witchcraft.

Munn, in his essay on shamanistic curing by the Mazatec Indians of Oaxaca, Mexico, is able, by means of a remarkable literary style, to convey something of the impact of such a hallucinogen-induced experience on a participating outsider. His investigations took place in Huautla de Jiménez, a village famous for its sacred usage of psychotropic mushrooms, especially *Psilocybe mexicana*. These fungi, which were also used in pre-Columbian Aztec ceremonies, contain the hallucinogenic indole-derived alkaloids psilocybine and psilocine (cf. Schultes, 1963: 159–162; Farnsworth, 1968: 1089; Hoffer and Osmund, 1967: 480–500; Heim, 1963; Wasson, 1958, 1961; Wasson and Heim, 1958; Wasson and Wasson, 1957).

In Munn's account we find the eternal dilemma of the participant observer revealed, like the experience itself, as an interaction between two worlds. In the case of hallucinogenic substances, the experience is compounded, for not only are there the usual two cultural worlds to be reconciled, but also the "ordinary" and "non-ordinary" realities (Castaneda, 1968). No one can write of participant observation in such situations completely "objectively"; it would be a disservice to pretend to be able to do so. Munn meets the problem head-on; he juxtaposes the shamans' communications with his own; all of them aided by the inspiration of the mushrooms. Munn, in addition, attempts analysis on a personal level in light of his own Western experience and knowledge. He is not an anthropologist; and thus is able to contribute something beyond the boundaries normally constricting ethnological investigation.

Munn conveys the persuasive reality of the hallucinogenic drug experience within a formally shamanistic context. In a sense, he has become a convert. He says, "To call such transcendental experiences of light, vision, and speech hallucinatory is to deny that they are revelations of reality." He suggests that the shaman's active participation in the group session through chant and communication of revelation results in an experience that "is intuitionary not hallucinatory." He further proposes that the chemical properties of the mushrooms especially activate centers of the brain connected with language and speaking. Thus, for him, the oracular features of Mazatec shamanism are direct results of the effects of the psychoactive mushrooms. He states, from his own experience, "At times it is as if one were being told what to say, for the words leap to mind, one after another, of themselves without having to be searched for: a phenomenon similar to the automatic dictation of the surrealists. . . ." If Munn is right, his observations raise interesting questions regarding the possible role of analogous chemical substances in promoting oracular behavior in other times and places. It has, for instance, long been claimed that chemical factors were operative in the case of the oracle at Delphi in ancient Greece, although the nature of the specific agents involved has been of some dispute.

5

Shamanism and Peyote Use Among the Apaches of the Mescalero Indian Reservation

L. Bryce Boyer, Ruth M. Boyer,
and Harry W. Basehart

In a volume devoted to the study of shamanism and hallucinogenic drugs it is important to include data concerning a group whose experiences with the hallucinogenic peyote cactus (*Lophophora williamsii*) in shamanistic rituals resulted in serious conflict and, ultimately, proscription of the ceremonial use of the drug.[1] In

1. An earlier version of this paper was presented at the Hallucinogens and Shamanism symposium at the annual meeting of the American Anthropological Association in 1968. The research which made this communication possible was supported in part by National Institute of Mental Health Grants M-2013 and M-3088 and University of California (Berkeley) Faculty Grants. It has continued since 1958. The ultimate purpose of the research is to delineate areas of interaction among social structure, socialization, and personality organization. Harry W. Basehart has been responsible for collecting data pertaining to social structure. He was assisted in 1959–60 by Bruce B. MacLachlan. Ruth M. Boyer has gathered socialization data and also aided Basehart. L. Bryce Boyer has studied personality organization. The principal psychological consultant was Bruno Klopfer; his assistants were Florence B. Brawer, Hayao Kawai, and Suzanna B. Scheiner. Basehart has spent more than a year on the reservation, MacLachlan over fourteen months, and the Boyers over two years.

L. BRYCE BOYER, M.D., RUTH M. BOYER, PH.D., and HARRY W. BASEHART, PH.D., have worked as an inter-disciplinary team in their studies of Mescalero Apache shamanism. L. Bryce Boyer is a practicing psychoanalyst in Berkeley, California, who in his considerable field research specializes in shamanism. Ruth M. Boyer is an anthropologist and Lecturer in the Department of Design at the University of California, Berkeley. Dr. Basehart is Professor of Anthropology at the University of New Mexico and Editor of the *Southwestern Journal of Anthropology*.

this contribution we present information concerning the Apaches of the Mescalero Indian Reservation, some of whom used peyote in shamanistic contexts between about 1870 until some time after 1910. We then examine some of the reasons why its use was abandoned and why their accredited shamanistic practices subsequently have excluded the use of hallucinogens.[2]

The Apaches presently living on the reservation include members of three tribes, in order of descending numbers, Mescaleros, Chiricahuas, and Lipans (R. M. Boyer, 1962, Appendix A). The reservation was established in 1873 for the Mescaleros. The Chiricahuas were taken as prisoners of war in 1886 after the capitulation of Geronomo and his followers. When they were freed in 1913, the majority chose to move to the reservation and to become part of the Mescalero tribe. The Lipans were destroyed as functioning groups during the latter half of the nineteenth century, when their few known remaining members joined the Mescaleros.

Nineteenth-century authors stated that the Mescaleros used peyote in religious rites in 1867 (Methvin, 1899:36–37), the Chiricahuas in 1875 (Jones, 1899:95), and the Lipans in 1885 (Havard, 1885:521; 1886:38). Nevertheless, it is not generally known that these Apaches ate peyote. They were excluded from Shonle's (1925) map of the distribution of the use of peyote in the United States and they were listed as non-users in a booklet compiled under the aegis of the Bureau of Indian Affairs (Newberne, 1925.) During his field work in the 1930's, Opler (1936) learned that the Mescaleros had practiced rather elaborate ceremonies centering on the utilization of peyote for some forty years and that the Lipans had used it in shamanistic contexts (Opler, 1938, 1940, 1945).

According to the aged informant Antonio Apache, the Lipans obtained peyote from the Carrizo Indians (Opler, 1938); and the Mescaleros are said to have learned peyote rites from the Lipans not long before 1870 (La Barre, 1938) or from the Tonkawas, Lipans, Yaquis, or other non-Apachean groups of northern Mexico (Opler, 1936:148). But for some slight degree of experimentation by today's young people with marijuana and perhaps LSD,

2. The Apaches call peyote *hoos*. Almost no one remembers an aboriginal name, *xucladjin-dei* (Castetter and Opler, 1936:61).

the reservation Apaches are not known to have used any other hallucinogenic drugs with the exception of alcohol. Modern informants affirm that peyote has been and may now be used for social purposes, but that formerly it was ingested only during Mescalero and Lipan shamanistic ceremonies. We have been unable to confirm its use during the years 1958–71. No one now has knowledge of peyote use by the Chiricahuas of the reservation.

To understand why the shamanistic use of peyote was abandoned requires an insight into Apache religious concepts and a cognizance of personality structure among these people. Initially we shall summarize the religious tenets.

Aboriginal religio-medical philosophies, the criteria for according the status of shaman to individuals, and shamanistic procedures have been similar if not identical among the three tribes in recorded times (Boyer, 1964). They conceive the world to be permeated by supernatural power which has no intrinsic attribute of good or evil; its virtue resides in its potency. Power approaches people through the agency of a plant, animal, or natural phenomenon by means of a dream or other hallucinatory experience; its acceptance is frequently accompanied by an ordeal. Ritual instruction may be received directly from the power or from other shamans. Any person is a possible power recipient. Thus, Opler (1936:146) described the Mescaleros as "a tribe of shamans, active or potentially active."

An individual might own any number of powers. If he is thought to use power for purposes which are not oriented toward the common good, he is accorded the status of witch. Yet those who are thought to use their powers for the benefit of the group, the shamans, are implicitly witches since a shaman who saves a life must then either sacrifice his own or that of a loved person. Obviously, jealousies, enmities, and suspicion abound. Each shaman has private instructions concerning the use of power, and his rites are individually owned. Consistent with native concepts of leadership and authority (Basehart, 1959, 1960, 1970), there has never been a chief shaman.

Opler's informants stated, and today's Apaches agree, that ritual peyote use was acquired from personal contact with power that approached people while it was invested in peyote flowers or "buttons." Various Mescalero shamans acquired peyote power and became leaders of a peyote camp in which curing and other ceremonies were conducted. During such rites, various shamans and other participants used and were affected by peyote, experiencing the usual perceptual and logical distortions, hallucinations, and physical effects. Whether the Lipans had a formal peyote camp is not known.

There is a fundamental incongruity between the principles involved in ordinary Mescalero shamanistic ceremonies and the rules that applied to peyote rites. In ordinary shamanistic practices, a single shaman is the principal figure and the experiences of attendants at ceremonies are subordinate. Religious ecstasy, visions, and communications with supernaturals are the shaman's prerogatives and validate his power and efficacy. The use of peyote by other people at ceremonies made its psychological and physiological effects common, and the uniqueness of the shaman's experiences disappeared. The peyote meetings became places in which shamanistic rivalries and witchcraft flourished. Disruption resulted, rather than cohesiveness through shared experience.

The peyote ceremonies were not accompanied by the acceptance of Christian beliefs and practices, and the Mescaleros never became involved in the Peyote Religion (see Slotkin, 1956). Instead, the use of peyote was intended to affirm the vitality of traditional religious practices at a time when the impact of reservation confinement contributed to an increased awareness of social and cultural deprivation. Yet antagonisms became so open and bloody that eventually the peyote gatherings were abandoned. The hostilities which became overt during the meetings were ascribed to the peyote. Since its use involved witchcraft practices, its ingestion was equated with the potential for witchcraft.

It will be recalled that, in the native conceptualization, power has no intrinsic attribute of good or evil, and can be used for moral or immoral purposes at the will of its human owner. To our knowledge, peyote power is unique among the Mescaleros in that it is *uniformly* considered to be bad. Some Mescaleros believe that one other power, the owl, is intrinsically evil. Thus, the hoot of an owl is considered to presage death. However, some Apaches regard the owl as the bearer of the power of a human witch, others believe ghosts to inhabit owls, and yet others deem owls to be witches whose actions are motivated by their own evil will or power.

During 1959–60 there were thirteen accredited Mescalero, Chiricahua, and Lipan shamans on the reservation. Perhaps fifteen Mescaleros, here termed pseudoshamans, claimed to own supernatural power but were considered generally to be imposters. One of the shamans, Ancient One, was the sole living person known to have participated in the peyote camp. Of the shamans, only he and Black Eyes (Boyer, 1961; Klopfer and Boyer, 1961), both Mescaleros, were at times judged to be witches. It was said that they and two of the pseudoshamans still used peyote in the illicit practices of witchcraft and love magic ceremonies, rites which are potentially dangerous to those who perform them. The shamans, considered to be legitimate possessors of peyote power, were not punished by that power for their actions. However, the peyote had "turned back" on the pseudoshamans. As a consequence, one of them lost one of his legs in an accident and the other was castigated indirectly when one of his close relatives was killed and another lost a limb.

Let us turn now to a brief and partial recapitulation of facets of current socialization practices. R. M. Boyer (1962) found that child-rearing techniques tend to be uniform in emotional content, and usually in actual practice, provided the mother has been brought up on the reservation. Further, during the prelatency period of a child's growth, socialization practices strongly resemble aboriginal tactics.

Typically, there is gross inconsistency in the maternal care of children. Frequently, the baby of the family is afforded tender and loving care but periodically the mother will impulsively abandon the infant to the supervision of others, sometimes to children of only four or five years of age, for hours or days while she engages in narcissistic pursuits, commonly involving drinking. Ordinarily, a husband does not object to such treatment of small children because his attention and regard are no more constant. Under such conditions, the development of a sense of basic trust (Erikson, 1950) is stultified; one result is the marked ambivalence and suspiciousness which form aspects of Apache personality.

With the birth of a baby, usually when the previous child is 18 to 24 months old, the older child is abruptly, and often brutally, displaced. The resultant sibling rivalry is intense but strongly disapproved. Nevertheless, its repression is insecure and its effects become blatantly manifest when teenagers and adults are under the influence of alcohol. We refer here to only two of the severe psychological traumata encountered by growing children.

In the aboriginal situation, other socialization practices were reasonably effective in directing hostilities engendered by such child-rearing practices, for example, those mentioned above toward outsiders, witches, ghosts and other culturally defined objects. During the long period when these Apaches were nomadic hunters, gatherers, and raiders, such externalization of aggression served to strengthen group solidarity. With changing life conditions, in the presence of feeble repression of intrafamilial and intragroup resentments, individuals' hatreds are generally discharged in manners which result in anomie and various forms of self-destruction (Boyer and Boyer, 1972).

L. B. Boyer's essential research method consisted of conducting psychoanalytically oriented investigative interviews (Boyer, 1964a). He had from 1 to 145 interviews each with 60 different persons of both sexes, ranging in age from 4 to 65 years. He found a personality configuration which was typical for these Apaches. They are impulse-ridden, fear loss of control, especially of feebly repressed hostile urges, and are suggestible and phobic. They tend to avoid introspection and seek outer controls and explanations for their behavior and thoughts. They are suspicious and dependent and their libidinal attachments are unstable. The men, who are caught between passive and aggressive urges, have insecure sexual identities. The typical Apache personality configuration corresponds with the Western psychiatric diagnosis of character disorder with hysterical and impulsive attributes.

L. B. Boyer was generally considered to be a shaman and,

accordingly, was in an unusually good position to learn about shamans and their activities. He found them to have personality configurations that concur with those which are typical for the Apaches, differing only to the degree to which they successfully employ imposture and in their having greater creative potential (Boyer, 1962).[3] They are not autocultural deviants who have resolved serious psychopathological conditions through assuming shamanistic roles (Ackerknecht, 1943; Devereux, 1956; Silverman, 1967). The personality structure of the imposter as delineated by psychoanalysts (Greenacre, 1958) is clinically similar to that of the usual Apache shaman.

A capacity to regress in the service of the ego (Kris, 1952) and an ego-controlled availability of primary process thinking (Freud, 1915) are related to creativity and showmanship. These characteristics appear to be necessary for the successful practice of shamanism and for convincing impostureship. It is noteworthy that the pseudoshamans who were interviewed were found clinically to lack creative potentials and the capacity to use regression in the service of the ego.

Because it was impossible to conduct psychiatric interviews in depth with all of the shamans and pseudoshamans, the Rorschach test was employed as a research adjunct. Protocols were obtained from all Apaches of fifty years of age and older (referred to here as the old-age group), 12 of the 13 shamans and 7 pseudoshamans (Boyer, Klopfer, Brawer, and Kawai, 1964). The protocols of the shamans and pseudoshamans were compared with those of the old-age group and with each other. As expected, the protocols of the old-age group showed hysterical signs. The shamans demonstrated more hysterical signs and, additionally, a way of handling data with keener awareness of peculiarities and more selective theoretical interest; they had creative characteristics and a high degree of reality testing potential in addition to a capacity to regress in the service of the ego. Viewed heteroculturally, or within Devereux's framework of the ideal psychological normal, they more

---

3. Subsequently, Boyer reviewed the relevant literature on shamanism and concluded that, cross-culturally, shamans have personality configurations similar to those exhibited by Apache practitioners (Boyer, 1964b).

Peyote (*Lophophora williamsii*)

nearly approached normality than did their culture mates.[4] The personality of the pseudoshamans was strikingly different. They were not hysterical, had variable degrees of reality testing potential, and impoverished personalities. Klopfer concluded from indirect data that the shamans were able to use imposture convincingly whereas pseudoshamans could not.

COMMENT

Historical and modern data provide some partial and tentative answers to the intriguing question of why the Mescaleros abandoned the use of peyote in shamanistic rituals and today forbid its use.

4. Devereux's (1956) stand has been frequently misunderstood. He held that shamans must be considered to be seriously neurotic or psychotic when compared with the *hypothetical* psychological normal. Boyer's viewpoint has been similarly misunderstood. Thus Handelman (1968) has stated that Boyer considers shamans to be psychologically abnormal, inferring therefrom that he deems them to be autocultural deviants, which is not true (Boyer, 1969).

Apache child-rearing practices engender much hostility. Aggression was and is addressed institutionally toward outsiders, witches, ghosts, and cultural bogies in an attempt to produce individual repression of hostile impulses originally directed toward familial and societal members. The effort was more effective aboriginally but has never been strikingly successful. In the past, as today, when individuals were under the influence of hallucinogens, including alcohol, their unstable repression of hateful impulses toward parent and sibling surrogates became blatantly overt and threatened tribal unity.

The use of peyote in the camps introduced a foreign element into Apache shamanistic procedures, the simultaneous assumption of authority by more than one practitioner. Each of them vied for supremacy of power and status. The physiopsychological effects of the hallucinogen reduced the efficacy of their repression of the hostilities which had resulted from their socialization experiences. The drug-induced regression resulted in their releasing aggression in its earlier, childish form, directly toward parent and sibling surrogates. Bloodshed and feuds occurred; the Apache wisely banned the peyote camps.

It would appear that the ascription of the quality of evil to peyote (power), an act which involved basic deviation from the conceptualization of power without intrinsic properties of good or evil, was intended to deny the presence of intragroup hostility. The use of peyote was proscribed for shamans; thenceforth it was employed by possessors of supernatural power solely in witchcraft rituals, as was owl power, and love magic practices.

It can be no coincidence that only peyote and owl power have been considered to be evil in themselves. In each instance, murderous wishes are projected onto the power in question.

The Mescaleros, Chiricahuas, and Lipans fear the use of peyote for two stated reasons: (1) it has an evil power which will drive them to do evil and (2) it causes hallucinations, that is, reduces their capacity to perceive and judge external reality accurately. There is fear of the visual aberrations and of the strange qualities of movement encountered. In the first case, intrapersonal asocial tendencies are projected onto the peyote. Sexual transgressions arouse little overt anxiety among these Apaches except when intergenerational incest has occurred, but they fear their poorly controlled aggressive impulses. The second case is similar. The Apaches may displace their fear of loss of control over destructive urges onto fear of loss of control of perceptual accuracy.

A number of questions remain, of which we shall deal briefly with three.

First, why did two shamans continue to use peyote in illicit practices? Both were considered to be very powerful and were feared by most Apaches. Black Eyes, intoxicated, frequently bragged that he was a witch and once flaunted peyote buttons before the psychoanalytic author. Ancient One had no need to flaunt his witchcraft potential. He was said to have killed many individuals, both tribal enemies and Apaches, sometimes by means which appeared to have required the intervention of the supernatural. His own children were so awed by his presumed powers that they even hesitated to whisper their conviction that he was a witch. Perhaps these two men deemed themselves to be so strong that they were above social sanctions and continued to use peyote both to demonstrate their contempt for their fellow Mescaleros and for material purposes. It is probable that they could demand greater recompense and command greater respect from performing rituals which were conceptualized as illegitimate in Apache practice and belief.

Second, why did two pseudoshamans use peyote in their rituals? They had impoverished personalities, and were generally scorned both as shamans and witches and employed solely by the most suggestible. We postulate that they used peyote in an attempt to raise their esteem in their eyes and those of others, hoping that they would truly become powerful if they could exploit the effects of the hallucinogens. Each of them confided to L. B. Boyer while intoxicated that they doubted their own claims of power possession and consciously sought to deceive others.

Third, the use of alcohol among these Apaches is commonplace. While it is officially and to some extent socially disapproved, it is accepted as "one way of life," a way accepted even prior to white domination. Under its influence, hallucinosis is frequent, and exceedingly violent actions often occur. Further, in the drunken state, perception is blurred and distorted, paralleling one aspect of the experiences induced by the ingestion of peyote. Why, then, was the use of alcohol socially permissible, while peyote was proscribed? A significant reason would appear to be the incorporation of peyote into the shamanistic ritual complex from the time of its introduction to the Apaches; the consumption of alcohol, to our knowledge, has never been culturally acceptable in ceremonial contexts. Where the group situation at peyote meetings fostered conflict centering on the varying powers controlled by and controlling particular individuals, aggression released during drinking parties was channeled outside the personally mediated world of the supernatural.

It will be most interesting to observe future Apache involvement with hallucinogens, inasmuch as their use has become commonplace among adolescents and young adults throughout the United States. Will the ban against the use of peyote extend to other hallucinatory agents with which Apaches may become familiar in their increasing intercourse with the world beyond the reservation? Or, might acquaintance with some hallucinogens pave the way for the re-definition of peyote, especially in view of the diminished commitment of the majority of present-day Apaches to the system of supernatural beliefs associated with shamanism? Research designed to answer these and related questions should yield significant data for cross-cultural comparison of processes of sociocultural change.

REFERENCES

Ackerknecht, E. H.
1943   Psychopathology, Primitive Medicine and Primitive Culture. *Bulletin of the History of Medicine* 14:30–67.
Basehart, H. W.
1959   *Chiricahua Apache Subsistence and Socio-Political Organization.* University of New Mexico Mescalero-Chiricahua Land Claims Project, Contract Research 290–154, mimeographed.
1960   *Mescalero Apache Subsistence Patterns and Socio-Political Organization.* Ibid.
1970   Mescalero Band Organization and Leadership. *Southwestern Journal of Anthropology* 26:87–106.

Boyer, L. B.
1961   Notes on the Personality Structure of a North American Indian Shaman. *Journal of the Hillside Hospital* 10:14–33.
1962   Remarks on the Personality of Shamans, with Special Reference to the Apaches of the Mescalero Indian Reservation. *The Psychoanalytic Study of Society* 2:233–54.
1964   Folk Psychiatry of the Apaches of the Mescalero Indian Reservation. *Magic, Faith and Healing. Studies in Primitive Psychiatry Today* (Ari Kiev, ed.), pp. 384–419. Glencoe, Ill.: The Free Press.
1964a Psychological Problems of a Group of Apaches: Alcoholic Hallucinosis and Latent Homosexuality among Typical Men. *Psychoanalytic Study of Society* 3:203–77.
1964b Further Remarks Concerning Shamans and Shamanism. *Israel Annals of Psychiatry and Related Disciplines* 2:235–57.
1969   Shamans: To Set the Record Straight. *American Anthropologist* 71:307–9.
Boyer, L. B., and Ruth M. Boyer
1972   Effects of Acculturation on the Vicissitudes of the Aggressive Drive among the Apaches of the Mescalero Indian Reservation. *Psychoanalytic Study of Society* 5:40–82.
Boyer, L. B., B. Klopfer, Florence B. Brawer, and H. Kawai
1964   Comparisons of the Shamans and Pseudoshamans of the Mescalero Indian Reservation. A Rorschach Study. *Journal of Projective Techniques and Personality Assessment* 28:173–80.
Boyer, Ruth M.
1962   *Social Structure and Socialization of the Apaches of the Mescalero Indian Reservation.* Unpublished Ph.D. dissertation, University of California, Berkeley.
Castetter, E. F., and M. E. Opler
1936   The Ethnobiology of the Chiricahua and Mescalero Apache. A. The Use of Plants for Foods, Beverages and Narcotics. *University of New Mexico Bulletin*, Vol. 4, No. 5.
Devereux, G.
1956   Normal and Abnormal: The Key Problem of Psychiatric Anthropology. *Some Uses of Anthropology: Theoretical and Applied*, pp. 23–48. Washington, D. C.: Anthropological Society of Washington.

Erikson, E. H.
   1950   *Childhood and Society*. New York: Norton.
Freud, S.
   1915   *The Unconscious. The Psychological Works of Sigmund Freud. Standard Edition*, 1957 (J. Strachey, ed.), Vol. 14, pp. 159–215. London: Hogarth Press.
Greenacre, Phyllis
   1958   The Imposter. *Psychoanalytic Quarterly* 27:359–82.
Handelman, D.
   1968   Shamanizing on an Empty Stomach. *American Anthropologist* 70:353–56.
Havard, V.
   1885   Report on the Flora of Western and Southern Texas. *Proceedings of the United States National Museum* 8:449–533.
   1886   Drink Plants of the North American Indians. *Bulletin of the Torrey Botanical Club* 23:33–46.
Jones, J. H.
   1899   *A Condensed History of the Apache and Comanche Indian Tribes*. San Antonio: Johnson.
Klopfer, B., and L. B. Boyer
   1961   Notes on the Personality Structure of a North American Indian Shaman: Rorschach Interpretation. *Journal of Projective Techniques* 25:170–78.
Kris, E.
   1952   *Psychoanalytic Explorations in Art*. New York: International Universities Press.
La Barre, W.
   1938   *The Peyote Cult*. New Haven: Yale University Press.
Methvin, J. J.
   1899   *Andele*. Louisville: Pentecostal Herald Press.
Newberne, R. E. L.
   1925   *Peyote*. Lawrence, Kansas: Haskell Institute.
Opler, M. E.
   1936   The Influence of Aboriginal Pattern and White Contact on a Recently Introduced Ceremony: The Mescalero Peyote Rite. *Journal of American Folk-Lore* 49:143–66.
   1938   The Use of Peyote by the Carrizo and Lipan Apache Tribes. *American Anthropologist* 40:271–85.
   1940   Myths and Legends of the Lipan Apache Indians. *Memoirs of the American Folk-Lore Society* 36:56–58.

1945 A Mescalero Apache Account of the Origin of the Peyote Ceremony. *El Palacio* 52:210–212.

Shonle, Ruth
1925 Peyote—Giver of Visions. *American Anthropologist* 27:53–75.

Silverman, J.
1967 Shamans and Acute Schizophrenia. *American Anthropologist* 69:21–31.

Slotkin, J. S.
1956 *The Peyote Religion.* Glencoe, Ill.: The Free Press.

6

Curing with Ayahuasca in an Urban Slum[1]

Marlene Dobkin de Rios

The use of plant hallucinogens in non-Western society has received widely scattered attention in the anthropological literature. Until recent years, however, there has been little attention paid to the important place that cultural variables such as belief systems, attitudes, and values have in determining and structuring one of the most subjective experiences available to anthropological inquiry.

This article, based on a year's fieldwork in the Peruvian Amazon city of Iquitos, will examine the role of cultural beliefs, attitudes, and values that are linked to the use of the plant hallucinogen *ayahuasca*—a drink made from cutting and boiling the woody vine several hours and used in Amazonian psycho-

1. This study was funded by the Foundations Fund for Research in Psychiatry, G67–395 (in collaboration with O. Rios Reategui). A debt of gratitude is acknowledged to Dr. Carlos Alberto Seguin, former Director of the Institute of Social Psychiatry, National University of San Marcos, Lima.

MARLENE DOBKIN DE RIOS, PH.D., is Research Anthropologist at the Metropolitan State Hospital, Norwalk, California, and Associate Professor of Anthropology at California State University, Fullerton. Her field research was in Peru, where she pursued studies, in collaboration with psychiatrists, of folk healing practices in towns of the North Coast and the Amazon basin. This essay is based upon findings embodied in her new book, *Visionary Vine: Psychedelic Healing in the Peruvian Amazon* (Dobkin de Rios, 1972a).

therapy sessions. A careful examination of such cultural variables as they enter into plant hallucinogenic use is an important but neglected dimension of the study of drug-induced altered states of consciousness. Such a focus on cultural determinants of hallucinatory experience should permit a more predictable index of collective visionary experience as it is found in scattered societies of the world, where such plants have been incorporated into religious and healing activity.

As psychologists have shown in clinical studies of hallucinatory phenomena, antecedent variables related to the drug phenomena must be examined. This is necessary to permit the prediction of clinical success in the treatment of psychoneurotic and emotional disease. Generally, clinicians attempt to specify the antecedent variables, consequent events, and antecedent-consequent relations as objectively as possible. By measuring the effects of such drugs in contemporary medical treatment, it is hoped that a theory of hallucinogenic drug effects can be developed (Barber, 1970:8ff).

The anthropologist who works in a natural laboratory situation where hallucinogens are used to treat disease cannot control the variables or even adequately measure dependent variables. The latter include somatic effects, reduced intellectual-motor proficiency, and changes in visual perception. Yet, such an investigation can delineate those cultural antecedent variables which contribute to the structuring of the experience itself. Clinical studies today tend to focus mainly upon non-cultural antecedent variables surrounding the administration of the drug, such as emotional atmosphere, and the subject's attitudes and motivations. Personality characteristics, too, are very much a part of the study. However, most if not all such clinical studies focus upon a pathological individual who receives the drug in a hospital or clinical setting. For the anthropologist studying drug use in a field situation, the measurement or control of the foregoing variables may be completely out of the question. Often the investigator is present during drug use by the gracious consent of a healer, who stands for little meddling with his ritual activities. What can anthropological analysis offer under these circumstances?

An anthropologist can focus upon the corpus of beliefs surrounding the group's use of hallucinogens—the cognitive system dealing with the belief in the drug's efficacy, the shared expectations of members of the community who expect to see certain visions and indeed report them in great frequency, and the actual nature and utilization of the insights and visions obtained in the hallucinogenically induced experiences.

Research Setting

In the Peruvian Amazon, there are ancient traditions of use of hallucinogens in religion, healing, and witchcraft activity. Today, in urban settings, *ayahuasca* has received its greatest cultural elaboration as an adjunct to folk healing. Mestizo healers in such urban centers as Iquitos and Pucallpa gather together groups of patients, ranging in number from five or six to as many as twenty-five, in clearings at the edge of these Amazonian cities. A drink made from boiling the *ayahuasca* vine several hours (and often containing additives besides various *Banisteriopsis* sps.)[2] is taken by the healer and most of his patients.

Healing sessions always occur at night. Patients gather in forest clearings with a healer (*ayahuasquero*), who conducts the drug ceremony. Healers carefully select their patients, tending to eliminate individuals who suffer from severe psychotic disorders. At about 10:00 p.m., the healer takes out a communal cup in which the *ayahuasca* potion is to be distributed. Reciting orations and whistling to protect each person who drinks, he passes the cup around the circle. He varies the amount of the potion in accordance with several factors, including his assessment of the patient's body weight, or physical strength. The optimal dose found by Rios Reategui was 7 mgm/kg of body weight (1962:48). My own impressions from the various sessions I attended was that the healer gave larger doses to persons suffering from psychosomatic illness—diseases with physical symptoms whose origin was believed by both to originate from some kind of magical harm.

2. Friedberg (1965:28) has delineated the major *Banisteriopsis* spp. in the Amazon region as *B. caapi*, *B. quitensis*, *B. inebriens*, and *B. rusbyana*. Additional plants which may be added to the brew include *toé*, identified by Schultes as *Datura suaveolens* (personal communication), and *chacruna* (*B. rusbyana*, the leaves of which contain dimethyltryptamine: see Der Marderosian, 1968).

Healers generally drink last, and an attempt is made by those present to reach a climax in their visions as close together as possible. People sit around smoking, and sometimes chatting for about half an hour, waiting for the effects of the potion to be felt. At times, someone may rise to vomit or defecate off to the side, but no effort is made to hide these sounds from those present. Healers use this time to stress the effectiveness of the purge (as *ayahuasca* is called because of side effects of vomiting or diarrhea) or to tell the patients how important it is that each person try to keep it in their stomachs as long as possible.

Healers use a good deal of Quechua[3] in their special drug songs during the ceremony. Whistling, too, marks many moments of the session and is interspersed throughout the evening's activities. As the hours pass, the healer moves around the circle contacting each person in turn, accompanied by his ever-present *schacapa* rattle (made by tying together dried leaves of a forest plant), which gives forth a rustling noise. During the curing ceremony, the healer blows cigarette smoke over the body of a sick person. If the patient is suffering pain, the healer may suck the dolorous area, bringing forth a spine or thistle, which those present believe was magically introduced by an enemy or evil spirit. Throughout the session, each person receives counseling and is ritually exorcised by the healer. At 2:00 a.m. or 3:00 a.m., after some four to five hours of strong drug intoxication, the patient returns to his home, unless he elects to spend the night in a nearby *tambo* (a wall-less shelter). Dietary proscriptions are an integral part of *ayahuasca* healing, because of a belief that the vine possesses a jealous guardian spirit. To propitiate this spirit, patients refrain from eating salt, lard, or sweets for at least 24 hours preceding and following the use of the purge. Sexual abstinence, too, may be demanded by the healer prior to the session.

Field Methodology

During the period June 1968–May 1969, I worked in the urban slum of Iquitos, called Belén, located on the Amazon River. This

3. The highland language of the Andean region.

community of some 12,000 people, dwelling in houses built on rafts, served as the source from which data on drug healers and patients were obtained, both categories being reputed to live in this community in large numbers.

Although my study was organized around the topic of *ayahuasca* use, I could not begin with a hypothesis since few published reports had appeared in the literature,[4] and the delineation of either basic ethnographic materials or cultural variables was completely lacking for all practical purposes. As a result, my main focus during the initial months of fieldwork was to gather data on beliefs about illness, as well as the role that *ayahuasca* played in Beleño society. As time passed I was able systematically to gather data on beliefs, values, and expectations concerning the plant's use.

Prior fieldwork in the North Coastal area of Peru gave me certain skills in the use of fortunetelling cards, locally called *naipes*. They served as an excellent method of obtaining data during fieldwork with *ayahuasca* (see Dobkin de Rios, 1969b). In January 1969, after several months of visiting the slum on a daily basis, I was able to set up a small consultation center in a local Beleño house. By telling fortunes, I obtained a reputation as a *curiosa*—a fortuneteller who charged a mere pittance for her services. Upon the advice of senior colleagues[5] I decided to charge a small amount of money (which was current practice for healers and fortunetellers) in order to make this service culturally valued. The funds thus obtained were used to purchase gifts of medicine and food, which were given regularly to slum residents. During the year's fieldwork in Belén, rapport was established with many slum families. I made gifts of black and white photographs to residents of the community, which in turn, facilitated invitations to festivals and funerals. Throughout daylight hours, I interviewed slum-dwellers and received clients who wished to know what the future held in store for them. Toward the end of my stay, I administered the Thematic Apperception Test. These findings were

4. See in particular Lemlij, 1965; Rios and Dobkin de Rios, 1967.

5. I wish to acknowledge in particular the good advice of Dr. Michael Harner and Dr. Ari Kiev for their encouragement in this somewhat unconventional anthropological method.

compared with the over 200 readings I had made of the *naipes* (see Dobkin de Rios, 1971).

The daily interviewing of Belén residents permitted me to gather data on either past or on-going use of *ayahuasca*, as well as facilitating introduction to several *ayahuasqueros*. During the course of the year, contact was established with ten healers and I observed several sessions. Most of the data on belief systems, however, were gathered from four healers willing to spend time with me discussing their activities.

In Belén, I found myself interviewing people who were neighbors but did not know one another. Nonetheless, there were striking similarities in the details they described of their *ayahuasca* treatment or their expectations of the drug's effect. To cross-check the data being gathered from direct interviewing, I paid particular attention to the card-reading materials. Various clients interpreted misfortune cards in light of illnesses they were experiencing. In this manner, I was able to verify data on the origins of disease with a second group whose contact with me had little to do directly with the use of *ayahuasca*. In addition, several sociological surveys had been made in this community in the past, and vital statistics were available in published form which I could cross-check with my own findings.[6]

After some months in the field, I took 100 micrograms of Sandoz LSD. At a later date, I also took *ayahuasca* in ritual context.[7] In most investigations of drug use, it is believed that the researcher must have some subjective experience in order to understand the nature of informants' reports. This was particularly applicable in the *ayahuasca* study, as culturally reported visions which filled notebooks seemed difficult to comprehend until a subjective experience clarified the veracity of reports about seeing unidentified persons appear in living color, etc. Recounting my own experience with *ayahuasca* provided an excellent entry into the world of informants' personal experience, since they were more apt to discuss their own visions with another person who had participated in their ritual.

The problem of sampling error is a difficult one to resolve,

6. See Wils, 1967; Oviedo, 1964; Grajeda, 1964.
7. The potion I received contained *B. caapi*, and *B. rusbyana* mixed together.

especially in the area of esoteric beliefs and practices. For one thing, although drug use (with the exception of *Cannabis*) is not illegal in Peru, practicing medicine without a license is. Thus, initial contacts with healers and attempts to gain their confidence often entailed not being terribly inquisitive nor asking too many questions. Being a woman in such a situation seemed to work to my advantage, for given the highly sex-typed roles present in slum life I did not appear to present any threat of revealing the healer's activities, especially since I came recommended by a family with whom I had an established friendship. When I returned to the United States and read Karsten's 1923 account of *ayahuasca* use among the Jívaro, located in the eastern Ecuadorian rain forest, almost 400 air miles away, I found his description of Jívaro belief systems linked to the spirit of the *ayahuasca* plant presented in very much the same language as one healer, don José, had used in Iquitos. This replication of data despite changes in time and space is the closest independent verification I can offer attesting to the persistence of *ayahuasca* use among disparate groups as the Jívaro and Iquitos mestizo populations of today.

Findings

Briefly summarizing ethnographic data on Belén,[8] we find that the slum serves as a receiving area for vast numbers of forest migrants who come to urban centers such as Iquitos in search of work and better schooling for their children. Slum life today has exceedingly high unemployment rates, excessive malnutrition, family breakdown, prostitution, vandalism, chronic illness, and a host of other social pathologies which set the stage for a different kind of social analysis from that available in community studies. Other urban slum analyses have focused upon networks of interacting dyadic relationships, finding structure within the amorphous structureless community. In an area like Belén, the fieldworker finds himself interacting with people who have little if any shared community tradition. Even the "amoral familiarism" that Banfield (1958) describes in South Italian communities does not enter

8. See Dobkin de Rios, 1972a, b, for more complete analyses of ethnographic data.

into the picture, as family unions are fragile things, with relationships between the sexes filled with tension and dissension. Elsewhere, data on elaborate systems of love magic prominent in this community have been explored in an attempt to relate such beliefs to the harsh economic facts of life (see Dobkin de Rios, 1969a).

Because of extreme economic insecurity resulting from lack of jobs, men and women work mainly at commercial activities tied to the movement of forest produce to the city market, which is located on an eroding palisade a few hundred feet above the slum community. Small-scale buying and reselling of vegetable or forest produce by slum residents who possess small amounts of capital are common occurrences. These wholesalers, called *rematistas*, fill the largest single occupational category in Belén. Some, more favored with accumulated capital, own motor-powered boats which are loaded with staples such as rice, sugar, coffee, and gasoline. These entrepreneurs, called *regatones*, ply the many river inlets selling their staples at a considerable mark-up to one-crop river hamlets. Forest peasants devote much of their time to activities such as hunting precious animal pelts to the neglect of agricultural activity, and thus provide the *regaton* with a steady market for the food staples.

The people of Belén live crowded together in an area that is flooded at least four months each year. During this time, houses are abandoned unless they are built on balsa log supports or on balsa rafts, which allows them to rise with the changing water level. Householders must use canoes to get to market or the city proper. Fishermen, in the past, earned their living in the nearby Itaya River. With growing populations, however, and indiscriminate fishing, natural resources have been fast disappearing. Fishing trips today often take men away from Belén for periods up to four to six weeks. Women are left behind, staying alive as best they can by reselling produce in the market. Their children often work at odd jobs to help out.

Causes of Disease

Among Beleños who live in an area of immense overcrowding, suffer from chronic underemployment, and are subject to high levels of malnutrition, disease is a constant companion. Informants describe various types of illness, some of which they consider to be simple and God-given. Colds, upper-respiratory infections, and some skin disorders can be easily treated, and poorly trained medical aides, called *sanitarios*, are frequent slum visitors who dispense penicillin or antibiotic injections for a small fee. Formal medical consultation in the city of Iquitos is far too costly for most slum residents, since an initial visit costs the equivalent of a two days' food budget for many. Moreover, the city hospital has the reputation as a place one goes in order to die, especially because of its casual way of dealing with poor people. When a simple fever, pain, or ache, however, does not respond well to an injection, tonic or other medicine, illness is frequently attributed to the malice of another person or to the punishment of a natural spirit. Perhaps a taboo has been broken by a person who has offended a spirit of nature. Thus, a menstruating woman who bathes before three days have passed, may hemorrhage because of the punishment of an offended forest spirit. Although many illnesses within tropical forest hamlet life are attributed to taboo violation, case histories collected in Belén focus in greater frequency upon the willing of evil by others. In this second category of magical illness, bewitchment occurs when an enemy consults a powerful witch who may then introduce a special preparation into someone's drink to cause harm or sickness. When city doctors or their medicine do not bring about an immediate recovery and when sudden aches or pains are felt in a particular part of the body, a resident of Belén is quite certain he has been bewitched.

As in many parts of the world where beliefs in magic, witchcraft and sorcery are auxiliaries to modern medicine, in Belén, one finds that the causal factors of illness are viewed primarily within a magical framework. Thus, the "why me?" and not the "how?" is the most frequent subject of inquiry into disease and all its ramifications. A person's concern upon becoming sick is to find out exactly why he and not someone else is afflicted. Nor are the answers simple ones, in light of on-going culture change, where twentieth century medical science has made certain inroads, most particularly in the area of pharmaceutical medicines and store-bought tonics used by many slum residents along with their magical treatments.

Most slum residents suffer from magical illnesses—those that afflict patients whose anxieties, fears, projections of hostility and hatred toward others—would propel them toward psychiatric help in Western medicine. Drug-healing in the Peruvian Amazon in many ways represents a very old and time-honored tradition of dealing with psychological problems that predates Freudian analysis by many centuries.

Magical Illnesses and Their Causes

Several major illnesses caused by the willing of evil by others are recognized by most urban slum residents. Once rapport has been established between anthropologist and informant, confidences are forthcoming in rapid succession about the malice to be found in the hearts of one's neighbors or relatives, who will often seek out a *brujo* (witch) to cause one harm. Most *ayahuasqueros* will acknowledge to the anthropologist that they are visited at one time or another by possible clients who may wish not only to be healed, but indeed, to cause harm to others. Some *ayahuasqueros* refuse this trade, but others are willing and specialize in the use of psychedelic drugs for socially defined evil purposes. They maintain that while intoxicated by the drug, they can leave their bodies and inflict harm and even incurable disease upon their clients' enemies.

The following are categories of illness elicited from informants in Belén:

SUSTO

A common illness found throughout Peru and Latin America, this infirmity includes cases of profound alteration of metabolism, or nervous disorder. *Susto* is an intense psychic trauma provoked by an emotion of fear and includes lack of appetite and energy. *Susto* is caused by the loss of the sick person's soul. This is one of the most frequent types of illness treated by Peruvian folk healers (see Sal y Rosas, 1958).

DAÑO

People say they suffer from *daño* because they are envied by others (*envidia*) or else because someone harbors feelings of vengeance toward them (*despecho*). Beleños recognize the important role that interpersonal strife and stress can play in generating such infirmities. *Daño* can be associated with a large number of illnesses, including hemorrhaging, muscular pain, loss of consciousness, suffocation, tumors, and consistent bad luck (called *saladera*). What is crucial here is the cause of such syndromes and not the actual manifestation of the disease.

It is believed that *daño* is caused either by means of a powerful potion which is slipped into a drink or else thrown across a doorstep late at night. A witch may be paid to cause magical harm to someone, by taking *ayahuasca* for such purposes. Some witches as well as *ayahuasqueros* are believed to control special spirits or familiars whom they can send to do evil or retribute evil magic. People believe that a *chonta* or thorn that carries disease-producing substances can be shot through the air by such witches at their enemies. As with all magical illness, it is imperative that a sick person suffering from *daño* seek a healer to neutralize the harm before it is fatal.

PULSARIO

An infirmity marked by symptoms of restlessness, hyperactivity, and free-floating anxiety, *pulsario* is sometimes described as a ball located at the mouth of the stomach which is painful and prevents normal digestive action. Attacking mainly women, *pulsario* is recognized by the fact that women become irritable and feel generally unhappy. Informants say that this lump can also be repressed pain, sorrow, or anger.

MAL DE OJO

Another disease syndrome found throughout Peru, *mal de ojo* is characterized by symptoms including nausea, vomiting, diarrhea, fever, loss of weight, insomnia, and sadness (Valdivia,

1964:84). In popular belief, the cause of the illness is the magical action of one person's glance upon the other, not necessarily with evil intentions in mind. *Mal de ojo*, however, can be motivated by envy. This illness is quite frequent among children whose personal attraction may catch the evil eye. Mothers often place charms or amulets on the wrist or neck of their youngsters or exorcise them each day with tobacco smoke in the belief they can ward off this disaster.

COMMENTS

The role of the *ayahuasquero* in healing such diseases is a central one. He must determine their origin before his patient can undergo any treatment. The healer must bring to light the cause of his patient's disease without the benefit of merely focusing upon a simple set of external symptoms. Once a sick person has found an *ayahuasquero* to treat him, both work closely together to analyze the visionary content of the drug experience to determine the agent responsible for the infirmity.

Ayahuasca Visions and Healing

One major pattern of informants' visions are reports of similar forest creatures such as boa constrictors and viperous snakes, which often appear before a man or woman taking *ayahuasca*. Although some people claim that *ayahuasca* causes no visual effects, most informants would tell of river and forest animals that fill their visions. Another frequent vision was that of the person responsible for bewitching them. Others would report a panorama of activity in which some man or woman would express his innermost thoughts and feelings toward the patient, such as sexual desire, vengeance, or hate. At times, some potion might be manufactured in a vision, which would later be thrown across a doorstep late at night.

As far as the viperous snakes and boa constrictors are concerned, these fearsome creatures, which in any part of the world might be considered part of a "bad trip" phenomenon, are rather cleverly utilized by healers to help them in their curing. Believed to be the reincarnated spirit of the vine itself, such mental productions are believed to bring messages of healing and assurance to the patient. If he is only strong enough to withstand the fright and loss of ego control when such apparitions appear, the mother spirit of the vine will teach him her songs. During a successful session, one can observe patients spontaneously breaking out into song, accompanying the healer or his apprentices.[9] Although the physiological effects of hallucinogenic use, ranging from states of euphoria to great anguish, probably have universal distribution (see Ludwig, 1969:13), it is quite interesting to note how such "bad trips" can be minimized or controlled by healing techniques when the presence of a belief system sets such activity within an ongoing magical framework. *Ayahuasca* use is harnessed in such a way that the effects of culturally acknowledged frightening mental productions are controllable by the healer and actually used by him to effect a cure. This is not to say that bad trips do not occur with *ayahuasca*. I observed some cases when individuals shrieked in fright as viperous snakes and assorted demons appeared before them.

Mechanisms of Healing

The use of *ayahuasca* to heal does not include a conceptualization of the hallucinogen as a curative agent, *per se*. Rather, the vine is seen to operate as a powerful means to a desired end—it gives the healer entry into the culturally important area of disease causality, enabling him to identify the nature of the illness from which a person is suffering and then to deflect or neutralize the evil magic which is deemed responsible for illness. When we examine the successes attributed to the healer, we find that in general terms, a selection process takes place so that curers accept patients only if they believe they will have a good chance of success. Simple illnesses are rarely treated with the drug, but herbs, plants, and store-bought medicines are prescribed by the healer for these types of affliction. Nor are psychotic patients given *ayahuasca*.

9. See Katz, 1971, for an excellent analysis of the *ayahuasca* whistling incantations and the important role they play in bridging two realms of consciousness.

In addition to the use of the vine, a healer will practice time-honored Amazonian curing traditions, including whistling, singing, recitation of orations, sucking at afflicted regions of the body, and blowing cigarette smoke over the body of the patient. *Ayahuasqueros*, like other regional folk healers who do not use drugs, spend a good portion of their time in afternoon consultations using the above techniques, as well as visiting homes of patients to advise, counsel, and reassure. Only patients suffering from certain types of illness take *ayahuasca*—usually those suffering from sickness often classified as psychosomatic.

The question arises in this kind of analysis: can we say that *ayahuasca* operates as a placebo? Is it possible that faith in the curative powers of the drug is enough to heal? It seems likely that we must dismiss this possibility. *Ayahuasca* is not used to gain verbal insight or to work through psychodynamic materials in order to effect long-range cures. Rather, the drug is used to identify the cause of magical illness. The generalized, immobilizing anxiety present in the sociocultural milieu is changed into solid fear placed squarely on the shoulders of some evil-doer by a healer whose presentation of self includes an omnipotent stance. Certainly, if an aura of personal success surrounds such a healer, it can only add to the patient's belief that such a man is powerful enough to counter any evil magic. The drug, then, serves mainly diagnostic and revelatory purposes throughout.

Magical Conditioning

As one historian of medicine pointed out, although irrational concepts of disease may be held in particular societies, nonetheless, many cures are effected (Gordon, 1949:65). It is interesting to examine mechanisms of healing in Iquitos, where patients are drawn from civilized or transitional Indian groups and from middle-income segments of the community who seek help from *ayahuasqueros* only after other "rational" techniques have failed. Because of this mixed grouping in a given *ayahuasca* session, a good healer, before allowing some of his patients to take the purge, will spend a period of up to two weeks exorcising the "evil" afflicting these individuals. This would seem to be a necessary part of the therapy, because of variant social realities. Magical beliefs among this latter segment function close to and at times in competition with rational ones. In order to alleviate anxiety generated by sensory overload inherent in drug ingestion, the healer in a series of subtle ways takes an omnipotent stance vis-à-vis his patients. Should there be any "doubting Thomas" present at the session, the possibility that the healer will be able to influence him while he is under the effects of the drug will be minimized. By means of the preparatory exorcistic rituals (which may include the use of a narcotic-like tobacco, possibly *Nicotiana tabacum*),[10] healers present some of their patients with a learning experience so as to permit them to come to terms with the culturally held expectations that they and others may have prior to a session. Patients' expectations, learned either in childhood or reinforced during these preliminary sessions, that they will be visited by a boa or other snake, as well as their belief in the curative prediction of success anticipated by that apparition's appearance, provide them with reassurance that healing is indeed occurring. In many ways, the omnipotence of the healer, which some writers see as crucial in explaining the efficacy of magical psychotherapies, is increased by the healer's symbolic presentations—his insistence upon the magical world of spirits that he controls, which he can conjure up through his particular songs and whistling incantations. At *ayahuasca* sessions, one often hears a healer advising a patient who is experiencing visions that the next song will cause such and such to happen, or that a difficult moment will pass. Called upon as a creative source to interpret the symbols that appear to his patients, the healer sees in these productions his own symbols which he attributes to magical causality of misfortune or disease.

Doctrinal Compliance

Ehrenwald (1966), tracing the continuity between present-day scientific therapy and primitive healing, coins the phrase "doctrinal compliance." He examines the phenomenon in Western psychotherapy that a patient ends up by doing what his doctor

10. See Janiger and Dobkin de Rios, n.d., for a discussion of the suggestive hallucinogenic properties of tobacco.

wants him to regardless of the particular school of allegiance to which a psychiatrist may subscribe. If a therapist, for example, is a Freudian, the patient's dreams often tend to re-create early memories of childhood or family conflict. At an unconscious level, then, the patient appears to be complying with the therapist's unconscious wishes and expectations in validating his theories. Unlike suggestion, which operates on a conscious level, doctrinal compliance seems to be an unconscious process which occurs in both magical and modern therapy procedures. This would seem to be very pertinent to the *ayahuasca* healing situation, especially with regard to the exorcising of the patient which marks a portion of contemporary healing in Iquitos.

Conclusion

The hallucinogen, *ayahuasca*, is used most effectively in healing those illnesses believed to be magical in origin. The particular visual hallucinations are put to use by the healer to determine the magical cause of illness as well as to neutralize evil magic. The importance of the forest setting, and the widespread knowledge, awareness, and familiarity of most people with the drug, the expectations of what will happen and the great respect for and remembered cures of drug healers, point up the importance of cultural variables stressed at the beginning of this article, which are of primary importance in understanding how hallucinogens have been used to augment healing.

The powerful vine, *ayahuasca*, is used quite differently from Western drug-adjuncted psychotherapy (see Caldwell, 1968). In the latter, attempts are made to open up areas of repressed and painful memories. Or else, long-term "psycholytic therapy" with drugs occurs, involving many months of treatment. Most *ayahuasca* healers see patients in a drug session for a relatively short period of time, which ranges from once or twice, to a month or so. Anxiety and stress which are constant companions of many rain forest slum-dwellers, can reach intolerable levels so that the drug healer receives a call to ameliorate acute symptoms. It is in these ritual, magical healing sessions that *ayahuasca* is used most effectively—entering into the realm of tenuous, uneasy interpersonal relations, and acting as a means to restore equilibrium in difficult situations.

REFERENCES

Banfield, Edward
  1958 *The Moral Basis of a Backward Society.* New York: The Free Press.
Barber, Theodore X.
  1970 *LSD, Marijuana, Hypnosis and Yoga.* Chicago: Aldine Publishing Company.
Caldwell, W. V.
  1968 *LSD Psychotherapy: An Exploration of Psychedelic and Psycholytic Therapy.* New York: Grove Press.
Der Marderosian, A. H., H. V. Pinkley, and M. F. Dobbins IV
  1968 Native Use and Occurrence of N,N-dimethyltryptamine in the Leaves of *Banisteriopsis rusbyana. American Journal of Pharmacy* 140:137–47.
Dobkin de Rios, Marlene
  1969a La cultura de la pobreza y la magia de amor: un síndrome urbano en la selva peruana. *América Indígena* 29:1 (January).
  1969b Fortune's Malice: Divination, Psychotherapy and Folk Medicine in Peru. *Journal of American Folklore* 82:132–41.
  1971 A Note on the Use of Ethno-tests and Western Projective Tests in a Peruvian Amazon Slum. *Human Organization* 30:89–94.
  1972a *Visionary Vine: Psychedelic Healing in the Peruvian Amazon.* San Francisco: Chandler Publishing Co.
  1972b *The Use of Hallucinogenic Substances in Peruvian Amazonian Folk Healing.* Unpublished Ph.D. dissertation, University of California, Riverside.
Ehrenwald, Jan
  1966 *Psychotherapy: Myth or Method.* New York: Grune and Stratton.
Friedberg, Claudine
  1965 Des Banisteriopsis utilisés comme drogue en Amérique du Sud. *Journal d'Agriculture Tropicale et de Botanique Appliquée* 12:9–12. Paris.

Gordon, Benjamin
    1949   *Medicine throughout Antiquity.* Philadelphia: Saunders.
Grajeda, Oscar
    1964   *Estudio socio-económico de Belén.* Iquitos: Universidad
            Nacional de la Amazonía Peruana.
Janiger, Oscar, and Marlene Dobkin de Rios
    n.d.   Suggestive Hallucinogenic Properties of Tobacco. Unpub-
            lished manuscript.
Karsten, Rafael
    1923   *Blood Revenge, War, and Victory Feasts among the Jibaro
            Indians.* Bureau of American Ethnology Bulletin 79, Smith-
            sonian Institution. Washington, D. C.
Katz, Fred, and Marlene Dobkin de Rios
    1971   Hallucinogenic Music: An Analysis of the Role of Whistling
            in Peruvian *Ayahuasca* Healing Sessions. *Journal of American
            Folklore* 84:320–27.
Lemlij, M., *et al.*
    1965   Del uso de psicodisléptico en la selva peruana. In *Perú,
            Sanidad del Gobierno y Policía.* Lima: Universidad Na-
            cional Mayor de San Marcos.
Ludwig, Arnold M.
    1969   Altered States of Consciousness. In Charles Tart (ed.),
            Altered States of Consciousness. New York: Wiley.
Oviedo, Jesus, *et al.*
    1964   *Estudio socio-económico de la Barriada del Puerto de Belén
            de la Ciudad de Iquitos.* Lima: Escuela de Servicio Social.
Rios, Oscar
    1962   Aspectos preliminares al estudio farmaco-psiquiátrico del
            Ayahuasca y su principio activo. *Anales de la Facultad de
            Medicina, Universidad Nacional Mayor de San Marcos.*
            Lima.
Rios, Oscar and Marlene Dobkin de Rios
    1967   Psychotherapy with Ayahuasca (a Harmine Drink) in N.
            Peru: Research Report and Proposal. *Transcultural Psy-
            chiatric Research* 4 (October).
Sal y Rosas, Federico
    1958   El mito de jani o susto de la medicina indígena del Perú.
            Revista de la Sanidad de Policía y Gobierno 18:167–210.
Valdivia, Oscar
    1964   *Historia de la psiquiatría peruana.* Lima: Universidad Na-
            cional Mayor de San Marcos.

Wils, Frits
  1967   *Estudio social sobre Belén—Iquitos.* Lima: Centro de In-
         vestigaciones Sociales, Económicas, Políticas y Antropo-
         lógicas.

7

The Mushrooms of Language

Henry Munn

The Mazatec Indians eat the mushrooms only at night in absolute darkness.[1] It is their belief that if you eat them in the daylight you will go mad. The depths of the night are recognized as the time most conducive to visionary insights into the obscurities, the mysteries, the perplexities of existence. Usually several members of a family eat the mushrooms together: it is not uncommon for a father, mother, children, uncles, and aunts to all participate in these transformations of the mind that elevate consciousness onto a higher plane. The kinship relation is thus the basis of the transcendental subjectivity that Husserl said is intersubjectivity. The mushrooms themselves are eaten in pairs, a couple representing

1. The Mazatec Indians, who have a long tradition of using the mushrooms, inhabit a range of mountains called the Sierra Mazateca in the northeastern corner of the Mexican state of Oaxaca. The shamans in this essay are all natives of the town of Huautla de Jiménez. Properly speaking they are Huautecans; but since the language they speak has been called Mazatec and they have been referred to in the previous anthropological literature as Mazatecs, I have retained that name, though strictly speaking, Mazatecs are the inhabitants of the village of Mazatlan in the same mountains.

HENRY MUNN has investigated the use of hallucinogenic plants among the Conibo Indians of eastern Peru and the Mazatec Indians of the mountains of Oaxaca, Mexico. Although not a professional anthropologist, he has resided for extended periods of time among the Mazatecs and is married to the niece of the shaman and shamaness referred to in this essay.

Psilocybe mexicana Heim. One of the most widely used psychotropic mushrooms of the Mazatec Indians of Oaxaca, Mexico.

man and woman that symbolizes the dual principle of procreation and creation. Then they sit together in their inner light, dream and realize and converse with each other, presences seated there together, their bodies immaterialized by the blackness, voices from without their communality.

In a general sense, for everyone present the purpose of the session is a therapeutic catharsis. The chemicals of transformation, of revelation that open the circuits of light, vision, and communication, called by us mind-manifesting, were known to the American Indians as medicines: the means given to men to know and to heal, to see and to say the truth. Among the Mazatecs, many, one time or another during their lives, have eaten the mushrooms, whether to cure themselves of an ailment or to resolve a problem; but it is not everyone who has a predilection for such extreme and arduous experiences of the creative imagination or who would want to repeat such journeys into the strange, unknown depths of the brain very frequently: those who do are the shamans, the masters, whose vocation it is to eat the mushrooms because they are the men of the spirit, the men of language, the men of wisdom. They are individuals recognized by their people to be expert in such psychological adventures, and when the others eat the mushrooms they always call to be with them, as a guide, one of those who is considered to be particularly acquainted with these modalities of the spirit. The medicine man presides over the session, for just as the Mazatec family is paternal and authoritarian, the liberating experience unfolds in the authoritarian context of a situation in which, rather than being allowed to speak or encouraged to express themselves, everyone is enjoined to keep silent and listen while the shaman speaks for each of those who are present. As one of the early Spanish chroniclers of the New World said: "They pay a sorcerer who eats them [the mushrooms] and tells them what they have taught him. He does so by means of a rhythmic chant in full voice."

The Mazatecs say that the mushrooms speak. If you ask a shaman where his imagery comes from, he is likely to reply: I didn't say it, the mushrooms did. No mushroom speaks, that is a primitive anthropomorphization of the natural, only man speaks, but he who eats these mushrooms, if he is a man of language, becomes endowed with an inspired capacity to speak. The shamans who eat them, their function is to speak, they are the speakers who chant and sing the truth, they are the oral poets of their people, the doctors of the word, they who tell what is wrong and how to remedy it, the seers and oracles, the ones possessed by the voice. "It is not I who speak," said Heraclitus, "it is the logos." Language is an ecstatic activity of signification. Intoxicated by the mushrooms, the fluency, the ease, the aptness of expression one becomes capable of are such that one is astounded by the words that issue forth from the contact of the intention of articulation with the matter of experience. At times it is as if one were being told what to say, for the words leap to mind, one after another, of themselves without having to be searched for: a phenomenon similar to the automatic dictation of the surrealists except that here the flow of consciousness, rather than being disconnected, tends to be coherent: a rational enunciation of meanings. Message fields of communication with the world, others, and one's self are disclosed by the mushrooms. The spontaneity they liberate is not only perceptual, but linguistic, the spontaneity of speech, of fervent, lucid discourse, of the logos in activity. For the shaman, it is as if existence were uttering itself through him. From the beginning, once what they have eaten has modified their consciousness, they begin to speak and at the end of each phrase they say *tzo*—"says" in their language—like a rhythmic punctuation of the said. Says, says, says. It is said. I say. Who says? We say, man says, language says, being and existence say.[2]

Cross-legged on the floor in the darkness of huts, close to the fire, breathing the incense of copal, the shaman sits with the furrowed brow and the marked mouth of speech. Chanting his words, clapping his hands, rocking to and fro, he speaks in the night of chirping crickets. What is said is more concrete than ephemeral phantasmagoric lights: words are materializations of consciousness; language is a privileged vehicle of our relation to reality. Let us go looking for the tracks of the spirit, the shamans say. Let us go to the cornfield looking for the tracks of the spirits' feet in the warm ground. So then let us go walking ourselves along the path in search of significance, following the words of two discourses enregistered like tracks on magnetic tapes, then translated from the native tonal language, to discover and explicitate what is said by an Indian medicine man and medicine woman during such ecstatic experiences of the human voice speaking with rhythmic force the realities of life and society.

The short, stout, elderly woman with her laughing moon face, dressed in a *huipil*, the long dress, embroidered with flowers and birds, of the Mazatec women, a dark shawl wrapped around her shoulders, her gray hair parted down the middle and drawn into two pigtails, golden crescents hanging from her ears, bent forward from where she knelt on the earthen floor of the hut and held a

2. The inspiration produced by the mushrooms is very much like that described by Nietzsche in *Ecce Homo*. Since the statement of Rimbaud, "I is another," spontaneous language, speaking or writing as if from dictation (to use the common expression for an activity very difficult to describe in its truth) has been of paramount interest to philosophers and poets. Says the Mexican, Octavio Paz, in an essay on Breton, "The inspired one, the man who in truth speaks, does not say anything that is his: from his mouth speaks language." Octavio Paz, "André Breton o La Busqueda del Comienzo," *Corriente Alterna* (Mexico: Siglo Veintiuno, 1967), p. 53.

handful of mushrooms in the fragrant, purifying smoke of copal rising from the glowing coals of the fire, to bless them: known to the ancient Meso-Americans as the Flesh of God, called by her people the Blood of Christ. Through their miraculous mountains of light and rain, the Indians say that Christ once walked—it is a transformation of the legend of Quetzalcoatl—and from where dropped his blood, the essence of his life, from there the holy mushrooms grew, the awakeners of the spirit, the food of the luminous one. Flesh of the world. Flesh of language. In the beginning was the word and the word became flesh. In the beginning there was flesh and the flesh became linguistic. Food of intuition. Food of wisdom. She ate them, munched them up, swallowed them and burped; rubbed ground-up tobacco along her wrists and forearms as a tonic for the body; extinguished the candle; and sat waiting in the darkness where the incense rose from the embers like glowing white mist. Then after a while came the enlightenment and the enlivenment and all at once, out of the silence, the woman began to speak, to chant, to pray, to sing, to utter her existence:[3]

> My God, you who are the master of the whole world, what we want is to search for and encounter from where comes sickness, from where comes pain and affliction. We are the ones who speak and cure and use medicine. So without mishap, without difficulty, lift us into the heights and exalt us.

From the beginning, the problem is to discover what the sickness is the sick one is suffering from and prognosticate the remedy. Medicine woman, she eats the mushrooms to see into the spirit of the sick, to disclose the hidden, to intuit how to resolve the unsolved: for an experience of revelations. The transformation of her everyday self is transcendental and gives her the power to move in the two relevant spheres of transcendence in order to

3. The shamanistic discourses studied in this essay, were tape-recorded. I am indebted for the translations to a bilingual woman of Huautla, Mrs. Eloina Estrada de Gonzalez, who listened to the recordings and told me, phrase by phrase, in Spanish, what the shaman and shamaness were saying in their native language. As far as I know, the words of neither of these oral poets have hitherto been published. They are Mrs. Irene Pineda de Figueroa and Mr. Román Estrada. The complete text of each discourse takes up ninety-two pages. For the purposes of this essay, I have merely selected the most representative passages.

achieve understanding: that of the other consciousness where the symptoms of illness can be discerned; and that of the divine, the source of the events in the world. Together with visionary empathy, her principal means of realization is articulation, discourse, as if by saying she will say the answer and announce the truth.

It is necessary to look and think in her spirit where it hurts. I must think and search in your presence where your glory is, My Father, who art the Master of the World. Where does this sickness come from? Was it a whirlwind or bad air that fell in the door or in the doorway? So are we going to search and to ask, from the head to the feet, what the matter is. Let's go searching for the tracks of her feet to encounter the sickness that she is suffering from. Animals in her heart? Let's go searching for the tracks of her feet, the tracks of her nails. That it be alleviated and healed where it hurts. What are we going to do to get rid of this sickness?

For the Mazatecs, the psychedelic experience produced by the mushrooms is inseparably associated with the cure of illness. The idea of malady should be understood to mean not only physical illness, but mental troubles and ethical problems. It is when something is wrong that the mushrooms are eaten. If there is nothing the matter with you there is no reason to eat them. Until recent times, the mushrooms were the only medicine the Indians had recourse to in times of sickness. Their medicinal value is by no means merely magical, but chemical. According to the Indians, syphilis, cancer, and epilepsy have been alleviated by their use; tumors cured. They have empirically been found by the Indians to be particularly effective for the treatment of stomach disorders and irritations of the skin. The woman whose words we are listening to, like many, discovered her shamanistic vocation when she was cured by the mushrooms of an illness: after the death of her husband she broke out all over with pimples; she was given the mushrooms to see whether they would "help" her and the malady disappeared. Since then she has eaten them on her own and given them to others.

If someone is sick, the medicine man is called. The treatment he employs is chemical and spiritual. Unlike most shamanistic methods, the Mazatec shaman actually gives medicine to his patients: by means of the mushrooms he administers to them physiologically, at the same time as he alters their consciousness. It is probably for psychosomatic complaints and psychological troubles that the liberation of spontaneous activity provoked by the mushrooms is most remedial: given to the depressed, they awaken a catharsis of the spirit; to those with problems, a vision of their existential way. If he hasn't come to the conclusion that the illness is incurable, the medicine man repeats the therapeutic sessions three times at intervals. He also works over the sick, for his intoxicated condition of intense, vibrant energy gives him a strength to heal that he exercises by massage and suction.

His most important function, however, is to speak for the sick one. The Mazatec shamans eat the mushrooms that liberate the fountains of language to be able to speak beautifully and with eloquence so that their words, spoken for the sick one and those present, will arrive and be heard in the spirit world from which comes benediction or grief. The function of the speaker, nevertheless, is much more than simply to implore. The shaman has a conception of *poesis*[4] in its original sense as an action: words themselves are medicine. To enunciate and give meaning to the events and situations of existence is life giving in itself.

"The psychoanalyst listens, whereas the shaman speaks," points out Lévi-Strauss:

> When a transference is established, the patient puts words into the mouth of the psychoanalyst by attributing to him alleged feelings and intentions; in the incantation, on the contrary, the shaman speaks for his patient. He questions her and puts into her mouth answers that correspond to the interpretation of her condition. A pre-requisite role—that of listener for the psychoanalyst and of orator for the shaman—establishes a direct rela-

4. ". . . the Greek word which signifies poetry was employed by the writer of an alchemical papyrus to designate the operation of 'transmutation' itself. What a ray of light! One knows that the word 'poetry' comes from the Greek verb which signifies 'make.' But that does not designate an ordinary fabrication except for those who reduce it to verbal nonsense. For those who have conserved the sense of the poetic mystery, poetry is a sacred action. That is to say, one which exceeds the ordinary level of human action. Like alchemy, its intention is to associate itself with the mystery of the 'primordial creation' . . ." Michel Carrouges, *André Breton et les données fondamentales du surréalisme* (Paris: Editions Gallimard, 1950).

tionship with the patient's conscious and an indirect relationship with his unconscious. This is the function of the incantation proper. The shaman provides the sick woman with a *language* by means of which unexpressed and otherwise inexpressible psychic states can be immediately expressed. And it is the transition to this verbal expression—at the same time making it possible to undergo in an ordered and intelligible form a real experience that would otherwise be chaotic and inexpressible—which induces the release of the physiological process, that is, the reorganization, in a favorable direction, of the process to which the sick woman is subjected.[5]

These remarks of the French anthropologist become particularly relevant to Mazatec shamanistic practice when one considers that the effect of the mushrooms, used to make one capable of curing, is to inspire the shaman with language and transform him into an oracle.

"That come all the saints, that come all the virgins," chants the medicine woman in her sing-song voice, invoking the beneficent forces of the universe, calling to her the goddesses of fertility, the virgins: fertile ones because they have not been sowed and are fresh for the seed of men to beget children in their wombs.

> The Virgin of Conception and the Virgin of the Nativity. That Christ come and the Holy Spirit. Fifty-three Saints. Fifty-three Saintesses. That they sit down at her side, on her mat, on her bed, to free her from sickness.

The wife of the man in whose house she was speaking was pregnant and throughout the session of creation, from the midst of genesis, her language as spontaneous as her being that has begun to vibrate, she concerns herself with the emergence of life, with the birth of an existence into that everyday social world that her developing discourse expresses:

> With the baby that is going to come there is no suffering, says. It's a matter of a moment, there isn't going to be any suffering, says. From one moment to another it will fall into the world, says. From one moment to another, we are going to

5. Claude Lévi-Strauss, "The Effectiveness of Symbols," *Structural Anthropology* (Doubleday Anchor, 1967), pp. 193–95.

save her from her woe, says. That her innocent creature come
without mishap, says. Her elf. That is what it is called when it
is still in the womb of its mother. From one moment to another,
that her innocent creature, her elf come, says.

"We are going to search and question," she says, "untie and
disentangle." She is on a journey, for there is distanciation and going there, somewhere, without her even moving from the spot
where she sits and speaks. Her consciousness is roaming throughout existential space. Sibyl, seer, and oracle, she is on the track of
significance and the pulsation of her being is like the rhythm of
walking.

"Let us go searching for the path, the tracks of her feet, the
tracks of her nails. From the right side to the left side, let us look."
To arrive at the truth, to solve problems and to act with wisdom, it
is necessary to find the way in which to go. Meaning is intentional.
Possibilities are paths to be chosen between. For the Indian
woman, footprints are images of meaning, traces of a going to and
from, sedimented clues of significance to be looked for from one
side to the other and followed to where they lead: indicators of
directionality; signs of existence. The hunt for meaning is a
temporal one, carried into the past and projected into the future;
what happened? she inquires, what will happen? leaving behind
for what is ahead go the footprints between departure and arrival:
manifestations of human, existential ecstasis. And the method of
looking, from the right side to the left side, is the articulation of
now this intuition, fact, feeling or wish, now that, the intention of
speaking bringing to light meanings whose associations and further elucidations are like the discovery of a path where the contents to be uttered are tracks to be followed into the unexplored,
the unknown and unsaid into which she adventures by language,
the seeker of significance, the questioner of significance, the articulator of significance: the significance of existence that signifies with
signs by the action of speaking the experience of existence.

"Woman of medicines and curer, who walks with her appearance and her soul," sings the woman, bending down to the ground
and straightening up, rocking back and forth as she chants, divid-
ing the truth in time to her words: emitter of signs. "She is the
woman of the remedy and the medicine. She is the woman who

speaks. The woman who puts everything together. Doctor woman. Woman of words. Wise woman of problems."

She is not speaking, most of the time, for any particular person, but for everyone: all who are afflicted, troubled, unhappy, puzzled by the predicaments of their condition. Now, in the course of her discourse, uttering realities, not hallucinations, talking of existence in a communal world where the we is more frequent than the I, she comes to a more general sickness and aggravation than physical illness: the economic condition of poverty in which her people live.

"Let us go to the cornfield searching for the tracks of the feet, for her poorness and humility. That gold and silver come," she prays. "Why are we poor? Why are we humble in this town of Huautla?" That is the paradox: why in the midst of such great natural wealth as their fertile, plentiful mountains where waterfalls cascade through the green foliage of leaves and ferns, should they be miserable from poverty, she wants to know. The daily diet of the Indians consists of black beans and tortillas covered with red chili sauce; only infrequently, at festivals, do they eat meat. White spots caused by malnutrition splotch their red faces. Babies are often sick. It is wealth she pleads for to solve the problem of want.

The mushrooms, which grow only during the season of torrential rains, awaken the forces of creation and produce an experience of spiritual abundance, of an astonishing, inexhaustible constitution of forms that identifies them with fertility and makes them a mediation, a means of communion, of communication between man and the natural world of which they are the metaphysical flesh. The theme of the shamaness, mother and grandmother, woman of fertility, bending over as she chants and gathering the earth to her as if she were collecting with her hands the harvest of her experience, is that of giving birth, is that of growth. Agriculturalists, they are people of close family interrelationships and many children: the clusters of neolithic thatch-roofed houses on the mountain peaks are of extended family groups. The woman's world is that of the household, her concern is for her children and all the children of her people.

"All the family, the babies and the children, that happiness

come to them, that they grow and mature without anything be-
falling them. Free them from all classes of sickness that there are
here in the earth. Without complaint and with good will," she
says, "so will come well-being, will come gold. Then we will have
food. Our beans, our gourds, our coffee, that is what we want.
That come a good harvest. That come richness, that come well-
being for all of our children. All my shoots, my children, my
seeds," she sings.

But the world of her children is not to be her world, nor that
of their grandfathers. Their indigenous society is being transformed by the forces of history. Until only recently, isolated from
the modern world, the Indians lived in their mountains as people
lived in the neolithic. There were only paths and they walked
everywhere they went. Trains of burros carried out the principal
crop—coffee—to the markets in the plain. Now roads have been
built, blasted out of rock and constructed along the edges of the
mountains over precipices, to connect the community with the
society beyond. The children are people of opposites: just as they
speak two languages, Mazatec and Spanish, they live between
two times: the timeless, cyclical time of recurrence of the People
of the Deer and the time of progress, change and development of
modern Mexico. In her discourse, no stereotyped rite or traditional
ceremony with prescribed words and actions, speaking of everything, of the ancient and the modern, of what is happening to
her people, the woman of problems, peering into the future, recognizes the inevitable process of transition, of disintegration and
integration, that confronts her children: the younger generation
destined to live the crisis and make the leap from the past into the
future. For them it is necessary to learn to read and to write and
to speak the language of this new world and in order to advance
themselves, to be educated and gain knowledge, contained in
books, radically different from the traditions of their own society
whose language is oral and unwritten, whose implements are the
hoe, the axe, and the machete.

Also a book is needed, says. Good book. Book of good reading in Spanish, says. In Spanish. All your children, your creatures, that their thought and their custom change, says. For me

there is no time. Without difficulty, let us go, says. With tenderness. With freshness. With sweetness. With good will.

"Don't leave us in darkness or blind us," she begs the origins of light, for in these supernatural modalities of consciousness there are dangers on every hand of aberration and disturbance. "Let us go along the good path. The path of the veins of our blood. The path of the Master of the World. Let us go in a path of happiness." The existential way, the conduct of one's life, is an idea to which she returns again and again. The paths she mentions are the moral, physical, mental, emotional qualities typical of the experience of animated conscious activity from the midst of which spring her words: goodness, vitality, reason, transcendence, and joy. Seated on the ground in the darkness, seeing with her eyes closed, her thought travels within along the branching arteries of the blood-stream and without across the fields of existence. There is a very definite physiological quality about the mushroom experience which leads the Indians to say that by a kind of visceral introspec-tion they teach one the workings of the organism: it is as if the system were projected before one into a vision of the heart, the liver, lungs, genitals, and stomach.

In the course of the medicine woman's discourse, it is under-standable that she should, from astonishment, from gratitude, from the knowledge of experience, say something about the mush-rooms that have provoked her condition of inspiration. In a sense, to speak of "the mushroom experience" is a reification as absurd as the anthropomorphization of the mushrooms when it is said that they talk: the mushrooms are merely the means, in interaction with the organism, the nervous system, and the brain, of produc-ing an experience grounded in the ontological-existential possibili-ties of the human, irreducible to the properties of a mushroom. The experience is psychological and social. What is spoken of by the shamaness is her communal world; even the visions of her imagination must have their origin in the context of her existence and the myths of her culture. The subject of another society will have other visions and express a different content in his discourse. It would seem probable, however, that apart from emotional sim-ilarities, colored illuminations, and the purely abstract patterns of a universal conscious activity, between the experiences of individuals with differing social inherences, the common characteristic would be discourse, for judging by their effect the chemical constituents of the mushrooms have some connection with the linguistic centers of the brain. "So says the teacher of words," says the woman, "so says the teacher of matters." It is paradoxical that the rediscovery of such chemicals should have related their effects to madness and pejoratively called them drugs, when the shamans who used them spoke of them as medicines and said from their experience that the metamorphosis they produced put one into communication with the spirit. It is precisely the value of studying the use in so-called primitive societies of such chemicals that the way be found beyond the superficial to a more essential understanding of phenomena which we, with our limited conception of the rational, have too quickly, perhaps mistakenly, termed irrational, instead of comprehending that such experiences are revelations of a primordial existential activity, of "a power of signification, a birth of sense or a savage sense." [6] What are we confronted with by the shamanistic discourse of the mushroom eaters? A modality of reason in which the logos of existence enunciates itself, or by the delirium and incoherence of derangement?

"They are doing nothing but talk," says the medicine woman, "those who say that these matters are matters of the past. They are doing nothing but talk, the people who call them crazy mushrooms." They claim to have knowledge of what they do not have any experience of; consequently their contentions are nonsense: nothing but expressions of the conventionality the mushrooms explode by their disclosure of the extraordinary; mere chatter if it weren't for the fact that the omnipotent *They* forms the force of repression which, by legislation and the implementation of authority, has come to denominate infractions of the law and the code of health, the means of liberation that once were called medicines. In a time of pills and shots, of scientific medicine, the wise woman is saying, the use of the mushrooms is not an ana-

6. "In a sense, as Husserl says, philosophy consists of the restitution of a power of signification, a birth of sense or a savage sense, an expression of experience by experience which particularly clarifies the special domain of language." Maurice Merleau-Ponty, *Le Visible et l'invisible* (Paris: Editions Gallimard, 1964).

The Mushrooms of Language [99]

chronistic and obsolete vestige of magical practices: their power to awaken consciousness and cure existential ills is not any the less relevant now than it was in the past. She insists that it is ignorance of our dimension of mystery, of the wellsprings of meaning, to think that their effect is insanity.

"Good and happiness," she says, naming the emotions of her activized, perceptualized being. "They are not crazy mushrooms. They are a remedy, says. A remedy for decent people. For the foreigners," she says, speaking of us, wayfarers from advanced industrial society, who had begun to arrive in the high plazas of her people to experiment with the psychedelic mushrooms that grew in the mountains of the Mazatecs. She has an inkling of the truth, that what we look for is a cure of our alienations, to be put back in touch, by violent means if necessary, with that original, creative self that has been alienated from us by our middle-class families, education, and corporate world of employment.

"There in their land, it is taken account of, that there is something in these mushrooms, that they are good, of use," she says. "The doctor that is here in our earth. The plant that grows in this place. With this we are going to put together, we are going to alleviate ourselves. It is our remedy. He that suffers from pain and illness, with this it is possible to alleviate him. They aren't called mushrooms. They are called prayer. They are called well-being. They are called wisdom. They are there with the Virgin, Our Mother, the Nativity." The Indians do not call the mushrooms of light mushrooms, they call them the holy ones. For the shamaness, the experience they produce is synonymous with language, with communication, on behalf of her people, with the supernatural forces of the universe; with plenitude and joyfulness; with perception, insight, and knowledge. It is as if one were born again; therefore their patroness is the Goddess of Birth, the Goddess of Creation.

With prayers we will get rid of it all. With the prayers of the ancients. We will clean ourselves, we will purify ourselves with clear water, we will wash our intestines where they are infected. That sicknesses of the body be gotten rid of. Sicknesses of the atmosphere. Bad air. That they be gotten rid of, that they be removed. That the wind carry them away. For this is the doctor. For this is the plant. For this is the sorcerer of the light of day. For this is the remedy. For this is the medicine woman, the woman doctor who resolves all classes of problems in order to rid us of them with her prayers. We are going with well-being, without difficulty, to implore, to beg, to supplicate. Well-being for all the babies and the creatures. We are going to beg, to implore for them, to beseech for their well-being and their studies, that they live, that they grow, that they sprout. That freshness come, tenderness, shoots, joy. That we be blessed, all of us.

She goes on talking and talking, non-stop; there are lulls when her voice slows down, fades out almost to a whisper; then come rushes of inspiration, moments of intense speech; she yawns great yawns, laughs with jubilation, claps her hands in time to her interminable singsong; but after the setting out, the heights of ecstasy are reached, the intoxication begins to ebb away, and she sounds the theme of going back to normal, everyday conscious existence again after this excursion into the beyond, of rejoining the ego she has transcended:

We are going to return without mishap, along a fresh path, a good path, a path of good air; in a path through the cornfield, in a path through the stubble, without complaint or any difficulty, we return without mishap. Already the cock has begun to crow. Rich cock that reminds us that we live in this life.

The day that dawns is that of a new world in which there is no longer any need to walk to where you go. "With tenderness and freshness, let us go in a plane, in a machine, in a car. Let us go from one side to another, searching for the tracks of the fists, the tracks of the feet, the tracks of the nails."

It seemed that she had been speaking for eight hours. The seconds of time were expanded, not from boredom, but from the intensity of the lived experience. In terms of the temporality of clocks, she had only been speaking for four hours when she concluded with a vision of the transcendence that had become immanent and had now withdrawn from her. "There is the flesh of God. There is the flesh of Jesus Christ. There with the Virgin."

The most frequently repeated words of the woman are freshness and tenderness; those of the shaman, whose discourse we will now consider, are fear and terror: what one might call the emotional poles of these experiences. There is an illness that the Mazatecs speak of that they name fright. We say traumatism. They walk through their mountains along their arduous paths on the different levels of being, climbing and descending, in the sunlight and through the clouds; all around there are grottos and abysses, mysterious groves, places where live the *laá*, the little people, mischievous dwarfs and gnomes. Rivers and wells are inhabited by spirits with powers of enchantment. At night in these altitudes, winds whirl up from the depths, rush out of the distance like monsters, and pass, tearing everything in their path with their fierce claws. Phantoms appear in the mists. There are persons with the evil eye. Existence in the world and with others is treacherous, perilous: unexpectedly something may happen to you and that event, unless it is exorcised, can mark you for life.

The Indians say following the beliefs of their ancestors, the Siberians, that the soul is sometimes frightened from one, the spirit goes, you are alienated from yourself or possessed by another: you lose yourself. It is for this neurosis that the shamans, the questioners of enigmas, are the great doctors and the mushrooms the medicine. It is the task of the Mazatec shaman to look for the extravagated spirit, find it, bring it back, and reintegrate the personality of the sick one. If necessary, he pays the powers that have appropriated the spirit by burying cacao, beans of exchange, wrapped in the bark cloth of offerings, at the place of fright which he has divined by vision. The mushrooms, the shamans say, show: you see, in the sense that you realize, it is disclosed to you. "Bring her spirit, her soul," implores the medicine woman to whom we have just been listening. "Let her spirit come back from where it got lost, from where it stayed, from where it was left behind, from wherever it is that her spirit is wandering lost."

With just such a traumatic experience, began the shamanistic vocation of the man we will now study. In his late fifties, he has been eating the mushrooms for nine years. Why did he begin? "I began to eat them because I was sick," he said when asked.[7]

7. The story of how he began his shamanistic career, together with the information to follow about fright, payments to the mountains, and practices in relation to the hunt, are quotations from an interview with Mr. Román Estrada whom I

No matter how much the doctors treated me, I didn't get well. I went to the Latin American Hospital. I went to Córdoba as well. I went to Mexico. I went to Tehuacán and wasn't alleviated. Only with the mushrooms was I cured. I had to eat the mushrooms three times and the man from San Lucas, who gave them to me, proposed his work as a medicine man to me, telling me: now you are going to receive my study. I asked him why he thought I was going to receive it when I didn't want to learn anything about his wisdom, I only wanted to get better and be cured of my illness. Then he answered me: now it is no longer you who command. It is already the middle of the night. I am going to leave you a table with ground tobacco on it and a cross underneath it so that you learn this work. Tell me which of these things you choose and like the best of all, he said, when everything was ready. Which of these works do you want? I answered that I didn't want what he offered me. Here you don't give the orders, he replied; I am he who is going to say whether you receive this work or not because I am he who is going to give you your diploma in the presence of God. Then I heard the voice of my father. He had been dead for forty-three years when he spoke to me the first time that I ate the mushrooms: This work that is being given to you, he said, I am he who tells you to accept it. Whether you can see me or not, I don't know. I couldn't imagine from where this voice came that was speaking to me. Then it was that the shaman of San Lucas told me that the voice I was hearing was that of my father. The sickness from which I was suffering was alleviated by eating the mushrooms. So I told the old man, I am disposed to receive what it is that you offer me, but I want to learn everything. Then it was that he taught me how to suck through space with a hollow tube of cane. To suck through space means that you who are seated there, I can draw the sickness out of you by suction from a distance.

What had begun as a physical illness, appendicitis, became a traumatic neurosis. The doctors wheeled him into an operating room—he who had never been in a hospital in his life—and suffocated him with an ether mask. And he gave up the ghost while

---

questioned through an interpreter: the conversation was tape-recorded and then translated from the native language by Mrs. Eloina Estrada de Gonzalez, the niece of the shaman, who served as questioner in the interview itself.

they cut the appendix out of him. When he came to, he lay frightened and depressed, without any will to live, he'd had enough. Instead of recuperating, he lay like a dead man with his eyes wide open, not saying anything to anyone, what was the use, his life had been a failure, he had never become the important man he had aspired all his life to be, now it was too late; his life was over and he had done nothing that his children might remember with respect and awe. The doctors couldn't help him because there was nothing wrong with him physically; contrary to what he believed, he had survived the operation; the slash into his stomach had been sewn up and had healed; nevertheless, he remained apathetic and unresponsive, for he had been terrified by death and his spirit had flown away like a bird or a fleet-footed deer. He needed someone to go out and hunt it for him, to bring back his spirit and resuscitate him.

The medicine man, from the nearby village of San Lucas, whom he called to him when the modern doctors failed to cure him of the strange malady he suffered from, was renowned throughout the mountains as a great shaman, a diviner of destiny. The short, slight, wizened old man was 105 years old. He gave to his patient, who was suffering from depression, the mushrooms of vitality, and the therapy worked. He vividly relived the operation in his imagination. According to him, the mushrooms cut him open, arranged his insides, and sewed him up again. One of the reasons he hadn't recovered was his conviction that materialistic medicine was incapable of really curing since it was divorced from all cooperation with the spirits and dependence upon the supernatural.

In his imagination, the mushrooms performed another surgical intervention and corrected the mistakes of the profane doctor which he considered responsible for his lingering lethargy. He went through the whole process in his mind. It was as if he were operating upon himself, undoing what had been done to him, and doing it over again himself. The trauma was exorcised. By intensely envisioning with a heightened, expanded consciousness what had happened to him under anesthesia, he assumed at last the frightening event he had previously been unable to integrate into his experience. His physiological cure was completed psychologically; he was finally healed by virtue of the assimilative, creative powers of the imagination. The dead man came back to life, he wanted to live because he felt once again that he was alive and had the force to go on living: once exhausted and despondent, he was now invigorated and rejuvenated.

The cure is successful because not only is his spirit awakened, but he is offered another future: a new profession that is a compensation for his humble one as a storekeeper. The ancient wise man, on the brink of death, wants to transmit to the man in his prime, his knowledge. What he encounters is resistance. The other doesn't want to assume the vocation of shaman, he only wants to be cured, without realizing that the cure is inseparable from the acceptance of the vocation which will release him from the repression of his creative forces that has caused the neurosis with which he is afflicted. It is no longer you who command, he is told, for his impulse to die is stronger than his desire to live; therefore the counterforce, if it is to be effective, cannot be his: it must be the will of the other transferred to him. You are too far gone to have any say in the matter, the medicine man tells him, it is already the middle of the night. By negating the will of his patient, he arouses it and prepares him to accept what is being suggested to him.

He shows him the table, the tobacco, the cross: signs of the shaman's work. The table is an altar at which to officiate. When the Mazatecs eat the mushrooms they speak of the sessions as masses. The shaman, even though a secular figure unordained by the Church, assumes a sacerdotal role as the leader of these ceremonies. In a similar way, for the Indians each father of a family is the religious priest of his household. The tobacco, San Pedro, is believed to have powerful magical and remedial values. The cross indicates a crossing of the ways, an intersection of existential paths, a change, as well as being the religious symbol of crucifixion and resurrection. The shaman tells him to choose. Still the man refuses. You don't give the orders, says the medicine man, intent upon evoking the patient's other self in order to bring him back to life, the I who is another. Whether you want to or not, you are going to receive your diploma, he says, to incite him with the prospect of award and reputation. Living in an oral culture without writing, where the acquisition of skills is traditional, handed down from father to son, mother to daughter, rather than contained in books, for the Mazatecs wisdom is gained during the experiences produced by the mushrooms: they are experiences of vision and communication that impart knowledge.

Now he is spoken to. The inner voice is suddenly audible. He hears the call. He is told to accept the vocation of medicine man that he has hitherto adamantly refused. He cannot recognize this voice as his own, it must be another's; and the shaman, intent upon giving him a new destiny, sure of the talent he has divined, interprets for him from what region of himself springs the command he has heard. It is your father who is telling you to accept this work. A characteristic of such transcendental experiences is that family relationships, in the nexus of which personality is formed, become present to one with intense vividness. His super-ego, in conjunction with the liberation of his vitality, has spoken to him and his resistance is liquidated; he decides to live and accepts the new vocation around which his personality is reinte-grated: he becomes an adept of the dimensions of consciousness where live the spirits; a speaker of mighty words.

In his house, we entered a room with bare concrete walls and a high roof of corrugated iron. His wife, wrapped in shawls, was sitting on a mat. His children were there; his family had assembled to eat the mushrooms with their father; one or two were given to the children of ten and twelve. The window was closed and with the door shut, the room was sealed off from the outside world; nobody would be permitted to leave until the effect of what they had eaten had passed away as a precaution against the peril of derangement. He was a short, burly man, dressed in a reefer jacket over a tee shirt, old brown bell-bottomed pants down to his short feet, an empty cartridge belt around his waist. In daily life, he is the owner of a little store stocked meagerly with canned goods, boxes of crackers, beer, soda, candy, bread, and soap. He sits be-hind the counter throughout the day looking out upon the muddy street of the town where dogs prowl in the garbage between the legs of the passers-by. From time to time he pours out a shot glass of cane liquor for a customer. He himself neither smokes nor drinks. He is a hunter in whom the instincts of his people survive from the time when they were chasers of game as well as agricul-turalists: inhabitants of the Land of the Deer.

Now it is night-time and he prepares to exercise his shamanistic function. His great-grandfather was one of the counselors of the town and a medicine man. With the advent of modern medicine and the invasion of the foreigners in search of mushrooms, the shamanistic customs of the Mazatecs have almost completely vanished. He himself no longer believes many of the beliefs of his ancestors, but as one of the last oral poets of his people, he consciously keeps alive their traditions. "How good it is," he says, "to talk as the ancients did." He hardly speaks Spanish and is fluent only in his native language. Spreading out the mushrooms in front of him, he selected and handed a bunch of them to each of those present after blessing them in the smoke of the copal. Once they had been eaten, the lights were extinguished and everyone sat in silence. Then he began to speak, seated in a chair from which he got up to dance about, whirling and scuffling as he spoke in the darkness. It was pouring, the rain thundering on the roof of corrugated iron. There were claps of thunder. Flashes of lightning at the window.

> Christ, Our Lord, illuminate me with the light of day, illuminate my mind. Christ, Our Lord, don't leave me in darkness or blind me, you who know how to give the light of day, you who illuminate the night and give the light. So did the Holy Trinity that made and put together the world of Christ, Our Lord, illuminated the Moon, says; illuminated the Big Star, says; illuminated the Cross Star, says; illuminated the Hook Star, says; illuminated the Sandal, says; illuminated the Horse, says.

One who eats the mushroom sinks into somnolence during the transition from one modality of consciousness to another, into a deep absorption, a reverie. Gradually colors begin to well up behind closed eyes. Consciousness becomes consciousness of irradiations and effulgences, of a flux of light patterns forming and unforming, of electric currents beaming forth from within the brain. At this initial moment of awakenment, experiencing the dawn of light in the midst of the night, the shaman evokes the illumination of the constellations at the genesis of the world. Mythopoetical descriptions of the creation of the world are constant themes of these creative experiences. From the beginning, the vision his words create is cosmological. Subjective phenomena are given correlates in the elemental, natural world. One is not inside, but outside.

"This old hawk. This white hawk that Saint John the Evangelist holds. That whistles in the dawn. Whistles in the light of day. Whistles over the water." Wings spread wide, the annunciatory bird, image of ascent, circles in the sky of the morning, drifting on the wind of the spirit above the primordial terrain the speaker has begun to explore and delineate, his breathing, his inhalations and exhalations, as amplified as his expanded being: an explanation for the sudden expulsion of air, the whooshes and high-pitched, eerie whistles of the shamans on their transcendental flights into the beyond.

"Straight path, says. Path of the dawn, says. Path of the light of day, says." Through the fields of being there are many directions in which to go, existences are different ways to live life. The idea of paths, that appears so frequently in the shamanistic discourses of the Mazatecs comes from the fact that these originary experiences are creative of intentions. To be in movement, going along a path, is an expressive vision of the ecstatic condition. The path the speaker is following is that which leads directly to his destination, to the accomplishment of his purpose; the path of the beginning disclosed by the rising sun at the time of setting out; the path of truth, of clarity, of that revealed in its being there by the light of day.

"Where the tenderness of San Francisco Huehuetlan is, says. Where the Holy Virgin of San Lucas is, says. Where San Francisco Tecoatl is, says. San Geronimo Tecoatl, says." He begins to name the towns of his mountainous environment, to call the landscape into being by language and transform the real into signs. It is no imaginary world of fantasy he is creating, as those one has become accustomed to hearing of from the accounts of dreamers under the effects of such psychoactive chemicals, fabled lands of nostalgia, palaces, and jewelled perspectives, but the real world in which he lives and works transfigured by his visionary journey and its linguistic expression into a surreal realm where the physical and the mental fuse to produce the glow of an enigmatic significance.

"I am he who speaks with the father mountain. I am he who

speaks with danger, I am going to sweep in the mountains of fear, in the mountains of nerves." The other I announces itself, the transcendental ego, the I of the voice, the I of force in communication with force. His existence intensified, he posits himself by his assertions: I am he who. The simultaneous reference to himself in the first and third person as subject and object indicates the impersonal personality of his utterances, uttered by him and by the phenomena themselves that express themselves through him. Arrogantly he affirms his shamanistic function as the mediator between man and the powers that determine his fate; he is the one who converses with all connoted by *father*: power, authority, and origin. He is the one who is on familiar terms with the sources of fright. The conception of existence manifested by his words is one of peril, anxiety, and terror: experiences of which he has become knowledgeable by virtue of his own traumas, his life as a hunter, and his adventures into the weird, secret regions of the psyche. Where there is foreboding and trembling, the medicine man tranquilizes by exorcising the causes of disturbance. His work lies among the nerves, not in the underworld, but on the heights, places of as much anguish as the depths, where the elation of elevation is accompanied by the fear of falling into the void of chasms. This is perhaps why, throughout Central and South America, the conception of illness in the jungle areas is the paranoic one of witchcraft, whereas in the mountainous areas is prevalent the vertiginous idea of fright and loss of self.[8]

"There in Bell Mountain, says. There is the dirty fright. There is the garbage, says. There is the claw, says. There is the terror, says. Where the day is, says. Where the clown is, says. The Lord Clown, says." In vision he sees, throughout his being he senses a repulsive place of filth and contamination, a stinking site of pustulence, of rottenness and nausea, where lies a claw that might have dealt with cruel viciousness an infected wound. His words,

8. "Finally, the illness can be the consequence of a loss of the soul, gone astray or carried off by a spirit or a revenant. This conception, widely spread throughout the region of the Andes and the Gran Chaco, appears rare in tropical America." Alfred Métraux, "Le Chaman des Guyane et de l'Amazonie," *Religions et magies indiennes d'Amérique du Sud* (Paris: Editions Gallimard, 1967).

emanating evil, seem to insinuate some horrible deed that left an aftermath of guilt. The sinister hovers in the air. Where? Where the clown is, he says. Concern and carefreeness are linked together, dread and laughter, from which we catch an insight into the meaning of the matter: during such experiences of liberation, there are likely to be encountered disturbances of consciousness by conscience, when reflection comes into conflict with spontaneity, guilt with innocence. It is as if the self drew back in fright from its ebullience, from its forgetfulness, unable to endure its carefreeness for long without anxiety. But the exuberant welling up of forms is ceaseless, in this flux, this fountain, this energetic springing forth of life, the past is left behind for the future, all is renewed. Beyond good and evil is the playfulness of the creative spirit incarnated by the clown, character of fortuity, the laughing one with his gay science.

> Thirteen superior whirlwinds. Thirteen whirlwinds of the atmosphere. Thirteen clowns, says. Thirteen personalities, says. Thirteen white lights, says. Thirteen mountains of points, says. Thirteen old hawks, says. Thirteen white hawks, says. Thirteen personalities, says. Thirteen mountains, says. Thirteen clowns, says. Thirteen peaks, says. Thirteen stars of the morning.

The enumeration, by what seems to be a process of free association, of whirlwinds, clowns, personalities, lights, mountains, birds, and stars, is an expression of his ecstatic inventiveness. Whether he says what he sees or sees what he says, his activized consciousness is a whirlwind of imaginings and colored lights. Why always thirteen? Because twelve is many, but an even number, whereas thirteen is too many, an exaggeration, and signifies a multitude. What's more, he probably likes the sound of the word thirteen.

The mushroom session of language creates language, creates the words for phenomena without name. The white lights that sometimes appear in the sky at night, nobody knows what to call them. The mind activated by the mushrooms, from out of the center of the mystery, from the profoundest semantic sources of the human, invents a word to designate them by. The ancient wise men, to describe the kaleidoscopic illuminations of their shamanistic nights, drew an analogy between the inside and the outside and formed a word that related the spectrum colors created by the sunshine in the spray of waterfalls and the mists of the morning to their conscious experiences of ecstatic enlightenment: these are the whirlwinds he speaks of, gyrating configurations of iridescent lights that appear to him as he speaks, turned round and round and round himself by the turbulent winds of the spirit. Clowns are frequent personae of his discourse, the impish mushrooms come to life, embodiments of merriment, tumbling figments of the spontaneous performing incredible acrobatic feats, funny imaginations of joyfulness. Personalities are more serious. Others. Society. The faces of the people he knows appear to him, then disappear to be succeeded by the apparition of more people. The plurality of incarnated consciousnesses becomes present to him. Multitude. His is an elemental world where cruel, predatory birds wheel in the sky; where the star of the morning shines in the firmament. Outside the dark room where he is speaking, the mountains stand all around in the night.

> I am he who speaks with the dangerous mountain, says. I am he who speaks with the Mountain of Ridges, says. I am he who speaks with the Father, says. I am he who speaks with the Mother, says. Where plays the spirit of the day, says. Cold Water Mountain, says. Big River Mountain, says. Mountain of Harvest and Richness, says. Where the terror of the day is, says. Where is the way of the dawn, the way of the day, says.

It is significant that though the psychedelic experience produced by the mushrooms is of heightened perceptivity, the *I say* is of privileged importance to the *I see*. The utter darkness of the room, sealed off from the outside, makes any direct perception of the world impossible: the condition of interiorization for its visionary rebirth in images. In such darkness, to open the eyes is the same as leaving them closed. The blackness is alive with impalpable designs in the miraculous air. Even the appearances of the other presences, out of modesty, are protected by the obscurity from the too penetrating, revealing gaze of transcendental perception. Freed from the factuality of the given, the constitutive activity of consciousness produces visions. It is this aspect of such experiences, to the exclusion of all others, that has led them to be called hallucinogenic, without any attempt having been made to distinguish fantasy from intuition. The Mazatec shaman, however, instead of keeping silent and dreaming, as one would expect him to do if the experience were merely imaginative, talks. There are times when in the midst of his ecstasy, whistling and whirling about, he exclaims: "Look at how beautiful we're seeing!"—astonished by the illuminations and patterns he is perceiving—"Look at how beautiful we're seeing. Look at how many good things of God there are. What beautiful colors I see." Nevertheless, the *I am the one who speaks* enunciates an action and a function, weighted with an importance and efficacity which *I am the one who sees*, hardly more than an interjection of amazement, totally lacks.

"I am he who speaks. I am he who speaks. I am he who speaks with the mountains, with the largest mountains. Speaks with the mountains, says. Speaks with the stones, says. Speaks with the atmosphere, says. Speaks with the spirit of the day." For the Mazatecs, the mountains are where the powers are, their summits, their ranges, radiating with electricity in the night, their peaks and their edges oscillating on the horizons of lightning. To speak with is to be in contact with, in communication with, in conversation with the animate spirit of the inanimate, with the material and the immaterial. To speak with is to be spoken to. By a conversion of his being, the shaman has become a transmitter and receiver of messages.

"I am the dry lightning, says. I am the lightning of the comet, says. I am the dangerous lightning, says. I am the big lightning, says. I am the lightning of rocky places, says. I am the light of the dawn, the light of day, says." He identifies himself with the elements, with the crackle of electricity; superhuman and elemental himself, his words flash from him like lightning. Sparks fly between the synaptic connections of the nerves. He is illuminated with light. He is luminous. He is force, light, and rhythmic, dynamic speech.

The world created by the woman's words, articulating her experience, was a feminine, maternal, domestic one; the masculine discourse of the shaman evokes the natural, ontological world. "She is beseeching for you, this poor and humble woman," said the shamaness. "Woman of huipile, says. Simple woman, says. Woman who doesn't have anything, says." The man, conscious of his virility, announces: "I am he who lightnings forth."

"Where the dirty gulch is, says. Where the dangerous gulch is, says. Where the big gulch is, says. Where the fear and the terror are, says. Where runs the muddy water, says. Where runs the cold water, says." It is a landscape of ravines, mountains, and streams, he charts with his words, of physical qualities with emotional values: a terrain of being in its variations. He evokes the creation, the genesis of all things out of the times of mist; he praises, marvels, wonders at the world. "God the Holy Spirit, as he made and put together the world. Made great lakes. Made mountains. Look at the light of day. Look at how many animals. Look at the dawn. Look at space. Great earths. Earth of God the Holy Spirit." He whistles. The soul was originally conceived of as breath. The wind, he says, is passing through the trees of the forest. His spirit goes flying from place to place throughout the territory of his existence, situating the various locations of the world by naming them, calling them into being by visiting them with his words: where is, he says, where is, to create the geography of his reality. I am, where is. He unfolds the extensions of space around himself, points out and makes present as if he were there himself. "Where the blood of Christ is, says. Where the blood of the diviner is, says. Where the terror and the fright of day are, says. Where the superior lake is, says. Where the big lake is, says. There where large birds fly, says. Where fly dangerous birds." The world is not only paradisiacal in its being there, but frightening, with perils lurking everywhere. "Mountains of great whirlwinds. Where is the fountain of terror. Where is the fountain of fright." And the different places are inhabited by presences, by indwelling spirits, the gnomes, the little people. "Gnome of Cold Water, says. Gnome of Clear Water, says. Gnome of Big River, says. Big Gnome. Gnome of Burned Mountain. Gnome of the spirit of the day. Gnome of Tlocalco Mountain. Gnome of the Marking Post. White Gnome. Delicate Gnome."

The shaman, says Alfred Métraux, is "an individual who, in the interest of the community, sustains by profession an intermittent commerce with the spirits or is possessed by them." [9] According to the classical conception, derived from the ecstatic visionaries of Siberia, the shaman is a person who, by a change of his everyday consciousness, enters the metaphysical realms of the transcendental in order to parley with the supernatural powers and gain an understanding of the hidden reasons of events, of sickness and all manner of difficulty. The Mazatec medicine men are therefore shamans in every sense of the word: their means of inspiration, of opening the circuits of communication between themselves, others, the world, and the spirits, are the mushrooms that disclose, by their psychoactive power, another modality of conscious activity than the ordinary one. The mere eating of the mushrooms, however, does not make a shaman. The Indians recognize that it is not to everyone that they speak; instead there are some who have a longing for awakenment, a disposition for exploring the surrealistic dimensions of existence, a poet's need to express themselves in a higher language than the average language of everyday life: for them in a very particular sense the mushrooms are the medicine of their genius. Nonetheless, there is a very definite idea among the Mazatecs of what the medicine man does, and since the mushrooms are his means of converting himself into the shamanistic condition, the essential characteristics of this particular variety of psychedelic experience must be manifested by his activities.

"I am he who puts together," says the medicine man to define his shamanistic function:

he who speaks, he who searches, says. I am he who looks for the spirit of the day, says. I search where there is fright and terror. I am he who fixes, he who cures the person that is sick. Herbal medicine. Remedy of the spirit. Remedy of the atmosphere of the day, says. I am he who resolves all, says. Truly you are man enough to resolve the truth. You are he who puts together and resolves. You are he who puts together the personality. You are he who speaks with the light of day. You are he who speaks with terror.

9. Ibid.

It is immediately obvious that a discrepancy exists between the Indian conception of the mushrooms' effect and the ideas of modern psychology: whereas in experimental research reports they are said to produce depersonalization, schizophrenia, and derangement, the Mazatec shaman, inspired by them, considers himself endowed with the power of bringing together what is separated: he can heal the divided personality by releasing the springs of existence from repression to reveal the ecstatic life of the integral self; and from disparate clues, by the sudden synthesis of intuition, realize the solution to problems. The words with which he states what his work is indicate a creative activity neither outside of the realm of reason or out of contact with reality. The center of convergent message fields, sensitive to the meaning of all around him, he expresses and communicates, in direct contact with others through speech, an articulator of the unsaid who liberates by language and makes understood. His intuitions penetrate appearances to the essence of matters. Reality reveals itself through him in words as if it had found a voice to utter itself. The shaman is a signifier in pursuit of significance, intent upon bringing forth the hidden, the obscure into the light of day, the lucid one, intrepid enough to realize that the greatest secrets lie in regions of danger. He is the doctor, not only of the body, but of the self, the one who inquires into the origins of trauma, the interrogator of the familiar and mysterious. It is indeed as if that which he has eaten, by virtue of the possibilities it discovers to him, were of the spirit, for perception becomes more acute, speech more fluent, and the consciousness of significance is quickened. The mushrooms are a remedy to which one has recourse in order to resolve perplexities because the experience is creative of intentions. The way forth from the problematic is conceived of, the meaning of resolved. The shaman, he is the one in communication with the light and with the darkness, who knows of anxiety and how to dispel it: the man of truth, psychologist of the troubled soul.

Where is the fear, says. Where is the terror, says. Where stayed the spirit of this child, says. I have to search for it, says. I have to locate it, says. I have to detain it, says. I have to grab it, says. I have to call it, says. I have to whistle for it in the midst of terror, says. I have to whistle for it through the cumulus clouds. I have to whistle for it with the spirit of the day.

Once more there appears the notion of alienation, the malady of fright, the loss of the self. The task of the shaman, hunter of extravagated spirits, is to reassociate the disassociated. He explains his method himself in these words:

Under the effect of the mushrooms, the lost spirit is whistled for through space for the spirit is alienated, but by means of the mushrooms one can call for it with a whistle. If the person is frightened, the mushrooms know where his spirit is. They are the ones who indicate and teach where the spirit is. Thereby one can speak to it. The sick person then sees the place where his spirit stayed. He feels as if he were tied in that place. The spirit is like a trapped butterfly. When it is whistled for it arrives where one is calling it. When the spirit arrives in the person, the sick one sighs and afterwards is cleaned.

It becomes evident from the words used to describe the condition of fright—the spirit is said to have been left behind, to have stayed somewhere, to be tied up, and as we will see later, to be imprisoned—that just as in the etiology of the neuroses, the sickness is a fixation upon a traumatic past event which the individual is incapable of transcending and from which he must be liberated to be cured. It is not by chance that the mushrooms, which cause a flight of the spirit, should be considered the means of chasing what has flown away. The shaman goes in search; by empathic imagination, sometimes even by dialogue with the disturbed one, he gains an insight into the reasons for the state of shock, which allows him to make his invocations relevant to the individual case. The patient, by the mnemonic power of the mushrooms, freed from inhibitions and repressions, recalls the traumatic event, surmounts the repetition syndrome that perpetuates it by virtue of the ecstatic spontaneity that has been released from him, suffers a catharsis, and is brought back to life, integrated again.

Another method of regaining the lost spirit, used as well as invocation, is to barter for it. Merchants, the Mazatecs conceive of all transactions in terms of commerce, of trading one value for another. Throughout his discourse, the shaman, a storekeeper in daily life, dreams of money, of richness, of freedom from poverty. "Father Bank. Big Bank. Where the light of day is. Córdoba. Orizaba." He names the cities where the merchants of Huautla sell their principal commercial crop—coffee—in the market. "Where the Superior Bank is, says. Where the Big Bank is, says. Where the Good Bank is, says. Where there is money of gold, says. Where there is money of silver, says. Where there are big notes, says. Where the bank of gold is, says. Where the bank of well-being is, says." It is not surprising that among such mercantile people it should be considered possible to buy back the lost spirit, to retrieve it in exchange for another value.

"Where the fright of the spirit is. Going to pay for it to the spirit. Going to pay the day. Going to pay the mountains. Going to pay the corners." The shaman becomes a transcendental bargainer. He is told by the supernatural powers how much they demand as a ransom for the spirit they have expropriated, then he undertakes to transact the deal. He explains it himself in this way:

Cacao is used to pay the mountain and to pay for the life of the sick one. The Lord of the Mountain asks for a chicken. This is an important matter because it is the Masters of the Mountains who speak. That is the belief of the ancients. The chicken is the one who has to carry the cacao. Loaded with cacao it has to go and leave the offering in the mountain. Once it is on the mountain, seeing it loaded no one bothers to catch it because already it belongs to the Masters of the Mountain where it is lost forever. The cacao that it carries is money for the Master of the Mountain. The bark paper is used to wrap the bundle and the parrot feather that goes with it. The signification of the parrot feather is that it is as if the parrot himself arrived on the mountain. It is he who arrives announcing with his songs the arrival of the chicken loaded with cacao, the arrival of the money to pay what was asked for, as if the liberty of a prisoner were being paid for. It is as if an authority said to you, "This prisoner will be set free for a fine of one hundred pesos and if it isn't paid, he won't go free." The transaction probably has the psychological effect of assuaging anxiety with the assurance that the powers angered by a transgression have been appeased.

As we have seen, though these shamanistic chants are creations of language created by the individual creativity of the speakers, the structure of the discourses, short phrases articulated in succession terminated by the punctuation of the word *says*, tend to be similar from person to person, determined to a large extent by culture and tradition as is much of what is said. An instance is the invocatory reiteration of names, a characteristic common to all the Mazatec shamanistic sessions of speech. The names repeated by the Indian medicine men, devout Catholics, are those of the Virgin and the saints. In ancient times, other divinities must have been named, but without any doubt, to name and make present has always played a role in such chants. "Holy Virgin of the Sanctuary. Holy Virgin. Saint Bartholomew. Saint Christopher. Saint Manuel. Holy Father. Saint Vincent. Saint Mark. Saint Manuel. Virgin Guadalupe, Queen of Mexico." To sing out the holy names serves the function for the oral poet, like the stereotyped phrases of Homeric song, of keeping the chant going during the interludes of inspiration; at the same time, the rhythmic enunciation is a telling over of identities, an expression of the interpersonality of consciousness. To recall again the affirmation of Husserl: Transcendental subjectivity is intersubjectivity. The name is the word for the person. In the mind of the speaker one identity after another becomes present, names call up people, the vision of people calls up names. Instead of naming his own acquaintances, which might occur in a desacralized discourse, the shaman invokes the holy ones. The sacred nomenclature is a sublimation of the nomenclature of family and social relationships.

It is now his everyday self, his wife and his family whom he speaks about. "Our children are going to grow up and live. I see. I see my wife, my little working woman. I love her. I speak to her through space. I speak to her through the cumulus clouds. I call to her spirit. Nothing will befall us." Man and woman, the couple and their children, that is his theme now that love for his family wells up in his heart.

Nothing can happen to us. We will go on living. We will go on living in the company of my wife, of my people. We should not make our wife irritable. We went to receive her before God, in the sight of God, in the Sacred Sacrament, in sight of the altar. There was a great mass, there was a mass of union. We were able to respect each other forty-three days and therefore God disposed that our children should be born and live. Because of that our seeds bore fruit, our offspring grew, offspring and seed that God Our Lord gave us.

He who speaks and says, perhaps it is rumored that the work he is doing, this person, is great, that his ranch is large. He is not presumptuous. He is a humble person. He is a laborious person. He is a person of problems. He is a person who has already loaned his service as an authority. He has realized himself, his gifts are inherited, he is of important people: Justo Pastor, Juan Nazareno. He is of a great root, an important root. Large trees, old trees. All our children will live, says. Will have a good harvest. Will rear their animals. Well-being and pleasure in their sugar cane, in their coffee groves. I will live much time yet. I will become an old man with gray hair, I will continue living with my offspring and with my people. My children will have education and well-being. Education must be given to my sons.

He says the changes through which he passes, the transformations and permutations of his ecstatic consciousness in the course of its temporalization—the sense of gamble, the risks, the moments of fright, the presence of light and vigor. "It turns into a game of chance, says. It turns into terror, says. It turns into spirit, says."

He whistles and sings and dances about. "That which sounds is a harp in the presence of God and the Angel of the Guard. Plays space, plays the rocks, plays the mountains, plays the corners, plays fear, plays terror, plays the day." He plays the facets of the world as if they were musical instruments. Things and emotions, at the contact of his singing and touch are magically resolved into ringing vibrating tonalities, into music—music of mountains and rocks, of space and fear. "Where sound the trees, says. Where sound the rocks, says. Where sound baskets. Where sounds the spirit of the day." He is hearing the ringing and the buzzing and the humming of his effervescent consciousness and finding analogies for the sounds he hears in the echo chambers of his eardrums: the soughing of the wind through the trees, the clinking of stones, the creaking of baskets. He whistles and sings. His words issue forth from the melodic articulation of inarticulate sounds, from the physical movement of his rhythmic whirling about and scuffling in the darkness. "How beautiful I sing," he exclaims. "How beautiful I sing. How many good pleasures concedes to us the Lord of the World." He dances about working himself up to a further pitch of exaltation. "How beautiful I dance. How beautiful I dance." Repetition is one of the aspects of the discourse as it is of the pulsation of energy waves.

"This person is valiant," he says of himself. "He is of the people of Huautla, he is a Huautecan. With great speed he calls and whistles for the spirits among the mountains; whistles the fright of the spirit." Then he flips out. He throws himself into the shamanistic fit, his voice changes, becomes that of another, rougher, more guttural, and beginning to speak in the speech of San Lucas from where came his old master, a town in the midst of the corn on a high windswept peak, he recalls his spiritual ancestor, the ancient wise man who taught him the use of the gnomic mushrooms. "He is a person of jars. He is of San Lucas. A person of plates. He is a person of jars and bowls. He is an old one." San Lucas is the place where all the black, unadorned, neolithic pottery used throughout the region is made. Men go from town to town carrying the jars, padded with ferns, on their backs to sell them in the marketplaces of the mountain villages. "Old man of pots, dishes, bowls. These are the people of the center. They speak with the mountains arrogantly. He is from San Lucas. He speaks with the whirlwind, with the whirlwind of the interior."

From what he himself tells of this old shaman, appear vestiges of the days when the shaman of the People of the Deer, intermediary between man, nature, and the divine was a thaumaturge who presided over fertility and the hunt. "I had to visit the same medicine man," he recounts, "when we went to the hunt. I had to prepare for him an egg, an egg to be offered to the mountain. It all depends on the value of the animal that one wants. It is as if you were going to buy an animal," he said.

> He is the one who says what one is to pay. He goes to leave the egg. Afterwards the dogs go into the woods and begin to work. It is necessary to rub tobacco on the crown of the dogs' heads. But with the egg and twenty-five beans of cacao, the master is sure that the deer is already bought. I have paid for the game, says the true shaman. And every time we went to hunt, we were therefore sure to encounter deer because a good shaman from San Lucas can transform a tree or a stone into a deer once he has exchanged its value for it with the Lord of the Mountain. We were sure to come upon deer because they had been paid for.

"Here come the Huautecans. Here come the Huautecans." Dancing about in the darkness, flapping his coat against his sides to imitate the bounding of a startled deer through the underbrush, he, the hunter of spirits and of game, barking like the dogs closing in around the cornered animal, tells a hunting story, talking rapidly with intense excitement in the gruff voice of one from San Lucas who sees from his vantage point the hunters of Huautla in the distance:

> Listen to how their dogs bark. It's an old dog. Here they come by way of the Sad Mountain. They are bringing their kill. There is barking in the mountain. Here they come. Listen to how their arms sound. Already they have shot a colored deer. They pay the mountains. They pay the corners. The deer was killed because the Huautecans pay the price. They paid the spirit. Paid the Bald Mountain. Paid the Hollow Mountain. Paid the Mountain of the Spirit of the Day. Paid fifty pesos. You can't do just as you like. It is necessary to pay the White Gnome. The Huautecans are like clowns. They are carrying the deer off along the path. The rifles of the Huautecans are very fine. These people are important people. They know what they are doing. They know how to call the spirit. The Huautecans call their dogs by blowing a horn. Already the dogs are coming close.

The story comes almost at the conclusion of his discourse. The effect of the mushrooms lasts approximately six hours; usually it is impossible to sleep until dawn. In all such adventures, at the end, comes the idea of a return from where it is one has gone, the return to everyday consciousness. "I return to collect these holy children that served as a remedy," the shaman says, calling back his spirits from their flight into the beyond in order to become his ordinary self again. "Aged clowns. White clowns." The mushrooms he calls sainted children and clowns, relating them by his personifications to beings who are young and joyful, playful, creative, and wise.

"The aurora of the dawn is coming and the light of day. In the name of the Father, the Son, and the Holy Spirit, by the sign of the Holy Cross, free us Our Lord from our enemies and all evil. Amen."

What began in the depths of the night with the illumination of interior constellations in the spaces of consciousness ends with the arrival of the daylight after a night of continuous, animated speech. "I am he who speaks," says the Mazatec shaman.

I am he who speaks. I am he who speaks with the mountains. I am he who speaks with the corners. I am the doctor. I am the man of medicines. I am. I am he who cures. I am he who speaks with the Lord of the World. I am happy. I speak with the mountains. I am he who speaks with the mountains of peaks. I am he who speaks with the Bald Mountain. I am the remedy and the medicine man. I am the mushroom. I am the fresh mushroom. I am the large mushroom. I am the fragrant mushroom. I am the mushroom of the spirit.

The Mazatecs say that the mushrooms speak. Now the investigators[10] from without should have listened better to the Indian wise men who had experience of what they, white ones of reason, had not. If the mushrooms are hallucinogenic, why

10. It is necessary to express one's debt to R. Gordon Wasson, whose writings, the most authoritative work on the mushrooms, informed me of their existence and told me much about them. "We suspect," he wrote, "that, in its integral sense, the creative power, the most serious quality distinctive of man and one of the clearest participations in the Divine . . . is in some sort connected with an area of the spirit that the mushrooms are capable of opening." R. Gordon Wasson and Roger Heim, *Les Champignons hallucinogènes du Mexique* (Paris: Muséum National d'Histoire Naturelle, 1958). From my own experience, I have found that contention to be particularly true.

do the Indians associate them with communication, with truth and the enunciation of meaning? An hallucination is a false perception, either visual or audible, that does not have any relation at all to reality, a fantastical illusion or delusion: what appears, but has no existence except in the mind. The vivid dreams of the psychedelic experience suggested hallucinations: such imaginations do occur in these visionary conditions, but they are marginal, not essential phenomena of a general liberation of the spontaneous, ecstatic, creative activity of conscious existence. Hallucinations predominated in the experiences of the investigators because they were passive experimenters of the transformative effect of the mushrooms. The Indian shamans are not contemplative, they are workers who actively express themselves by speaking, creators engaged in an endeavor of ontological, existential disclosure. For them, the shamanistic condition provoked by the mushrooms is intuitionary, not hallucinatory. What one envisions has an ethical relation to reality, is indeed often the path to be followed. To see is to realize, to understand. But even more important than visions for the Mazatec shaman are words as real as the realities of the real they utter. It is as if the mushrooms revealed a primordial activity of signification, for once the shaman has eaten them, he begins to speak and continues to speak throughout the shamanistic session of ecstatic language. The phenomenon most distinctive of the mushrooms' effect is the inspired capacity to speak. Those who eat them are men of language, illuminated with the spirit, who call themselves the ones who speak, those who say. The shaman, chanting in a melodic singsong, saying *says* at the end of each phrase of saying, is in communication with the origins of creation, the sources of the voice, and the fountains of the word, related to reality from the heart of his existential ecstasy by the active mediation of language: the articulation of meaning and experience. To call such transcendental experiences of light, vision, and speech hallucinatory is to deny that they are revelatory of reality. In the ancient codices, the colored books, the figures sit, hieroglyphs of words, holding the mushrooms of language in pairs in their hands: signs of signification.

III

In the Traditional Western World

PSYCHOTROPIC drugs not only were of central importance in European witchcraft, but their use sheds light upon the relationship of such rites to shamanism. However, most persons seem unaware that the use of hallucinogens was once a common practice in Europe. One reason for this lack of knowledge is that their use was long associated with practices generally deemed to be heretical, which the Church, through its Inquisitorial agents, largely suppressed. A second reason is that only recently, through the reoccurrence of hallucinogenic drug use in our modern society, have we become aware of the importance of the botanical substances employed in ancient rituals.

Many of the sources referred to in the following pages are in Latin and are often obscure or inaccurately translated elsewhere. Accordingly, all material from sources bearing Latin titles in the bibliography has been translated into English especially for this paper, unless otherwise indicated.

8

The Role of Hallucinogenic
Plants in European Witchcraft

Michael J. Harner

A prevalent attitude among present-day historians and scholars of religion (e.g., Henningsen, 1969: 105–6; Trevor-Roper, 1969: 90, 192) is that late medieval and Renaissance witchcraft was essentially a fiction created by the Church. Those taking this position often argue that the Inquisition had an *a priori* conception of witchcraft and simply tortured accused persons until they gave the "right" answers in terms of Church dogma. To support their position, they point out that many of the things witches confessed to doing, such as flying through the air and engaging in orgies with demons at Sabbats, were patently impossible.

The position of such scholars is not contravened by accounts of the rituals practiced by persons organized into formal witchcraft covens in Europe and the United States today. Such "witches" engage in what they think are the traditional practices, but insofar as I have been able to discover through interviews, do not believe that they fly through the air nor frolic with supernatural creatures at Sabbats. Instead, their activities tend to be sober and highly ritualistic. Academicians as well as present-day coven participants

A preliminary version of this paper was read at the Hallucinogens and Shamanism symposium at the annual meeting of the American Anthropological Association in Seattle in 1968. I am indebted to Lawrence Rosenwald and Philip Winter for assistance in making translations for this paper.

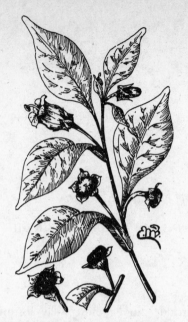

Deadly nightshade (*Atropa belladonna*)

Henbane (*Hyoscyamus*)

Mandrake (*Mandragora*)

Thorn apple (*Datura*)

have generally failed to comprehend the great importance of hallucinogenic plants in the European witchcraft of former times.[1]
Yet once the use and the effects of these natural hallucinogens are
understood, the major features of past beliefs and practices suddenly seem quite logical and consistent.

Probably the single most important group of plants used by
mankind to contact the supernatural belongs to the order Solanaceae (the potato family). Hallucinogenic members of this group
are widespread in both the Old and New Worlds. Besides the
potato, tomato, chile pepper, and tobacco, the family includes a
great number of species of the genus *Datura*, which are called by
a variety of names, such as Jimson weed, devil's apple, thorn
apple, mad apple, the devil's weed, Gabriel's trumpet, and angel's
trumpet, and are all hallucinogenic. *Datura* has been used widely
and apparently from ancient times in shamanism, witchcraft, and
the vision quest in Europe, Asia, Africa, and among American
Indian tribes. Other hallucinogens in the potato family closely
resembling *Datura* in their effects include mandrake (*Mandragora*), henbane (*Hyoscyamus*), and belladonna, or deadly nightshade (*Atropa belladonna*). Plants of this group are found in
both temperate and tropical climates, and on all continents.

Each of these plants contains varying quantities of atropine and
the other closely related tropane alkaloids hyoscyamine and scopol-
amine, all of which have hallucinogenic effects (Claus and Tyler,
1965: 273–85; Henry, 1949: 64–92; Hoffer and Osmund, 1967:
525–28; Lewin, 1964: 129–40; Sollmann, 1957: 381–98). These alkaloids can be extremely dangerous in their mental and physical
effects, and their toxicity can result in death.

One outstanding feature of atropine is that it is absorbable
even by the intact skin; and it has not been unusual in medicine
to observe toxic effects produced by belladonna plasters (Sollmann,
1957: 392). This potential of atropine-containing solanaceous

1. An important and essentially ignored exception was the distinguished nineteenth-century anthropologist Edward B. Tylor (1924 [orig. 1871]: vol. 2:418),
who proposed: ". . . the mediaeval witch-ointments . . . brought visionary beings
into the presence of the patient, transported him to the witches' sabbath, enabled
him to turn into a beast." More recent exceptions include Barnett (1965) as well as
Baroja (1964:255), the latter acknowledging that the effects of such ointments were
of fundamental importance, at least with regard to the witches' flight.

plants has long been known to man, both in the Old and New Worlds, and it is of considerable significance for the study of shamanism and witchcraft.

As is familiar to every child in our culture, the witch is fantasized as flying through the air on a broomstick. This symbol actually represents a very serious and central aspect of European witchcraft, involving the use of solanaceous hallucinogenic plants. The European witches rubbed their bodies with a hallucinogenic ointment containing such plants as *Atropa belladonna*, *Mandragora*, and henbane, whose content of atropine was absorbable through the skin. The witch then indeed took a "trip": the witch on the broomstick is a representation of that imagined aerial journey to a rendezvous with spirits or demons, which was called a Sabbat.

Lewin (1964 [orig. 1924]: 129–30), the famous pharmacologist, writes:

> We find these plants associated with incomprehensible acts on the parts of fanatics . . . Magic ointments or witches' philtres procured for some reason and applied with or without intention produced effects which the subjects themselves believed in, even stating that they had intercourse with evil spirits, had been on the Brocken and danced at the Sabbat with their lovers, or caused damage to others by witchcraft. The mental disorder caused by substances of this kind, for instance *Datura*, has even instigated some persons to accuse themselves before a tribunal. The peculiar hallucinations evoked by the drug had been so powerfully transmitted from the subconscious mind to consciousness that mentally uncultivated persons . . . believed them to be reality.

Hesse (1946: 103) writes in a similar vein of admixtures to witches' brew, love potions, and narcotics: "The hallucinations are frequently dominated by the erotic moment. . . . In those days, in order to experience these sensations, young and old women would rub their bodies with the 'witches' salve,' of which the active ingredient was belladonna or an extract of some other solanaceae."

The Inquisition, at the cost of the torture and execution of perhaps hundreds of thousands of believed and real witches, has supplied the bulk of our data on the role of hallucinogenic plants in late medieval Europe. From the variety of sources, only some of which are cited here, it is clear that we are dealing with practices that were widespread throughout Europe and apparently known at least as early as Roman times.

Margaret Murray is among the first modern scholars, after Tylor, to touch upon the possible importance of the "flying ointment" in European witchcraft. She notes (Murray, 1962 [orig. 1921]: 101–2) that the Somerset witches in 1664 used a "greenish" oil in transporting themselves to their meetings. Murray, following Glanvil (1681), (p. 304) observes:

> Elizabeth Style said:
> "Before they are carried to their meetings, they anoint their Foreheads and Hand-wrists with an Oyl the Spirit brings them (which smells raw) and then they are carried in a very short time, using these words as they pass, *Thout, tout a tout, tout, throughout and about*. And when they go off from their Meetings, they say, *Rentum, Tormentum* . . . all are carried to their several homes in a short space." Alice Duke gave the same testimony, noting besides that the oil was greenish in colour. Ann Bishop, the Officer of the Somerset covens, confessed that "her Forehead being first anointed with a Feather dipt in Oyl, she hath been suddenly carried to the place of their meeting. . . . After all was ended, the Man in black vanished. The rest were of a sudden conveighed to their homes."

Another case of the use of an ointment, three centuries earlier, is from an investigation by the authorities of Lady Alice Kyteler in 1324 (Murray, 1962 [orig. 1921]: 104, following Holinshed, 1587).

> . . . in rifleing the closet of the ladie, they found a Pipe of oyntment, wherewith she greased a staffe, upon the which she ambled and galloped through thick and thin, when and in what manner she listed.

The fifteenth century yields a similar account of an anointed staff:

> But the vulgar believe, and the witches confess, that on certain days or nights they anoint a staff and ride on it to the ap-

pointed place or anoint themselves under the arms and in other hairy places and sometimes carry charms under the hair. [Bergamo, *c.* 1470–71, *in* Hansen, 1901: 199]

The use of a staff or broom was undoubtedly more than a symbolic Freudian act, serving as an applicator for the atropine-containing plant to the sensitive vaginal membranes as well as providing the suggestion of riding on a steed, a typical illusion of the witches' ride to the Sabbat.

In addition to brooms, pitchforks and apparently baskets and bowls served as "vehicles" for transport to the Sabbat:

> Nicole Ganette added that it was her custom, when she was preparing to start on that journey, to put one foot up into a basket after she had smeared it with the same ointment which she had used upon herself. Francis Fellet said that he used to place his left foot, not in a basket, but on the ends of the backward bent twigs of a broom which he first anointed. [Remy, 1596, Liber I, Ch. xiv, p. 103]

Johannes Nider (1692, Liber II, Cap. 41) gives this account:

> I shall . . . show how so many people are deceived in their sleep, that upon wakening they altogether believe that they have actually seen what has happened only in the inner part of the mind. I heard my teacher give this account: a certain priest of our order entered a village where he came upon a woman so out of her senses that she believed herself to be transported through the air during the night with Diana and other women. When he attempted to remove this heresy from her by means of wholesome discourse she steadfastly maintained her belief. The priest then asked her: "Allow me to be present when you depart on the next occasion." She answered: "I agree to it and you will observe my departure in the presence (if you wish) of suitable witnesses." Therefore, when the day for the departure arrived, which the old woman had previously determined, the priest showed up with trustworthy townsmen to convince this fanatic of her madness. The woman, having placed a large bowl, which was used for kneading dough, on top of a stool, stepped into the bowl and sat herself down. Then, rubbing ointment on herself to the accompaniment of magic incantations she lay her head back and immediately fell asleep. With the labor of the devil she dreamed of Mistress Venus and other superstitions so

vividly that, crying out with a shout and striking her hands about, she jarred the bowl in which she was sitting and, falling down from the stool seriously injured herself about the head. As she lay there awakened, the priest cried out to her that she had not moved: "For Heaven's sake, where are you? You were not with Diana and as will be attested by these present, you never left this bowl." Thus, by this act and by thoughtful exhortations he drew out this belief from her abominable soul.

Vincent (MS., *c.* 1475, *in* Hansen, 1901: 229, 230) also suggests the utilization of hallucinogens in order to be "carried" to the Sabbats:

The devil casts people into deep sleep, in which they dream that they have been to the Sabbat, adored the demon, caused lightnings and hail-storms, destroyed vineyards, and burnt alive children taken from their mothers.

The malefici have philtres and unguents with which they poison or make sick, and they also imagine themselves to be carried to the Sabbat by virtue of these.

Remy, in the late sixteenth century, provides the following additional information:

For they have heard the evidence of those who have smeared and rubbed themselves with the same ointment that witches use, and have in a moment been carried with them to the Sabbat; though in returning it was a journey of many days. [Remy, 1596, Liber I, Ch. xiv, p. 92]

Bertranda Barbier admitted that she had often done this; namely, in order to lull her husband into such a sleep, she had many times tweaked his ear after having with her right hand anointed it with the same ointment which she used upon herself when she sought the journey to the Sabbat. [Remy, 1596, Liber I, Ch. xii, p. 83]

Now if witches, after being aroused from an "iron" sleep, tell of things they have seen in places so far distant as compared with the short period of their sleep, the only conclusion is that there has been some unsubstantial journey like that of the soul. [Remy, 1596, Liber I, Ch. xiv, p. 101]

Spina (1523, Cap. II, init.) gives this unusually detailed account:

First, indeed, there should be adduced the thing that happened to the illustrious Prince N., within the lifetime of those who are now alive. A certain witch, who said that she had often been carried on the journey, was being held in the prison of some cleric Inquistor. The Prince, hearing of this, desired to find out whether these claims were true or dreams. He summoned the Inquisitor D., and finally prevailed upon him to let the woman he brought forth and anoint herself with her usual ointment in their presence and in the presence of a multitude of nobles. When the Inquisitor had given his consent (even if in error), the witch asserted in their presence that, if she might anoint herself as before, she would go and be carried off by the Devil. Having anointed herself several times, however, she remained motionless; nor did anything extraordinary manage to happen to her. And many noble eye-witnesses of the matter survive to this very day. From this fact, it is obviously false that witches are carried on the ride as part of their pact; it is rather that when they think that they are so carried, it happens by a delusion of the Devil.

There are many other testimonies of this, and now it is my pleasure to adduce examples which are said to have happened in our own times. Dominus Augustinus de Turre, of Bergamo, the most cultivated physician of his time, told me a few years ago in his home at Bergamo, that when he was a youth at his studies in Padua, he returned home one night about midnight with his companions. He knocked, and when no one answered or opened the door, he climbed up a ladder and finally got into the house by a window. He went to look for the maid and finally found her lying in her room, supine upon the floor, stripped as if a corpse, and completely unconscious, so that he was in no way able to arouse her. When it was morning, and she had returned to her senses, he asked her what happened that night. She finally confessed that she had been carried on the journey; from which it is manifestly clear that they [witches] are deluded not bodily, but mentally or in dreams, in such a way that they imagine they are carried a long distance while they remain immobile at home.

Something similar to this last was told to me at Saluzzo a few years ago by Dr. Petrus Cella, formerly vicar of the Marchese of Saluzzo and still living: like things had happened to his own maidservant, and likewise he had discovered that she was deluded.

But there is also a story commonly told among us, that at the time when the Inquisition in the diocese of Como was being carried on by our people, in the walled city called Lugano, it happened that the wife of a notary of the Inquisition was accused by due process of law of being a witch and a sorceress. Her husband was exceedingly troubled at this, since he had thought her a holy woman. Then, through the will of the Lord, early on Good Friday, since he could not find his wife, he went to the pigsty. There he found her naked, in some corner, displaying her genitals, completely unconscious and smeared with the excrement of the pigs. Now then, made more certain of that which he had not been able to believe, he drew his sword in sudden wrath, wishing to kill her. Returning to himself, however, he stood waiting for a little while that he might see the outcome of all this. And lo, after a little while she returned to her senses. When she saw that her husband was threatening to kill her, she prostrated herself before him and, seeking pardon, promised that she would reveal the whole truth to him. So she confessed that she had gone that night on the journey, etc. Hearing these things, her husband left at once and made an accusation of her in the house of the Inquisitor, so that she might be given to the fire. She, however, though sought at once, was nowhere to be found. They think that she drowned herself in the lake above whose shore that area is situated.

A similar general statement is provided by Ciruelo in the early seventeenth century:

Witches, male and female, who have pact with the devil, anointing themselves with certain unguents and reciting certain words, are carried by night through the air to distant lands to do certain black magic. This illusion occurs in two ways. Sometimes the devil really carries them to other houses and places, and what they see and do and say there really happens as they report it. At other times they do not leave their houses, but the devil enters them and deprives them of sense and they fall as dead and cold. And he represents to their fancies that they go to other houses and places and do and see and say such and such things. But nothing of this is true, though they think it to be, and though they relate many things of what passes there. And while they are thus dead and cold they have no more feeling than a corpse and may be scourged and burnt; but after the time agreed upon with the devil he leaves them, their senses are liberated, they arise well and merry, relate what they have done and bring news from other lands. [Ciruelo, 1628, P. II, c. 1, N. 6, pp. 45–46]

The physician of Pope Julius III, Andrés Laguna, gives a similar account. In 1545, while he was practicing in Lorraine, a married couple was seized as witches, being accused of burning grain, killing livestock, and sucking the blood of children. Under torture, they confessed their guilt. Laguna reports:

> Among the other things found in the hermitage of the said witches was a jar half-filled with a certain green unguent, like that of Populeón [white poplar ointment], with which they were anointing themselves: whose odor was so heavy and offensive that it showed that it was composed of herbs cold [refers to the classification of medicines as "hot" and "cold"] and soporiferous in the ultimate degree, which are hemlock, nightshade, henbane and mandrake: of which unguent, by way of a constable who was my friend, I managed to obtain a good cannister-full which I later, in the city of Metz, used to anoint from head to toe the wife of the hangman, who because of suspicions about her husband was totally unable to sleep, and tossed and turned almost half mad. And this one seemed to be an appropriate subject on whom some tests could be made, since infinite other remedies had been tried in vain and since it appeared to me that it [the ointment] was highly appropriate and could not help but be useful, as one easily deduced from its odor and color. On being anointed, she suddenly slept such a profound sleep, with her eyes open like a rabbit (she also fittingly looked like a boiled hare), that I could not imagine how to wake her. By every means possible, with strong ligatures and rubbing her extremities, with affusions of oil of costus-root and officinal spurge, with fumes and smoke in her nostrils, and finally with cupping-glasses, I so hurried her that at the end of thirty-six hours she regained her senses and memory: although the first words she spoke were: "Why do you wake me at such an inopportune time? I was surrounded by all the pleasures and delights of the world." And casting her eyes on her husband (who was there all stinking of hanged men), she said to him, smiling: "Knavish one, know that I have made you a cuckold, and with a lover younger and better than you," and she said many other and very strange things. . . .

From all this we can conjecture that all that which the

Applying the ointment, in an engraving entitled *Departure for the Sabat*. The witch is astride her broomstick

Applying the ointment and the departure. In *The Witches' Kitchen*, Frans Francken's sixteenth-century painting of the demonic activities in a witches' kitchen, a young witch is rubbed down with flying ointment, and others disrobe for the same treatment (right). To the left, another witch flies up the chimney on her broomstick while other witches tend the cauldron amidst a muddle of demons.

wretched witches do is phantasm caused by very cold potions and unguents: which are of such a nature as to corrupt the memory and the imagination, that the wretched ones imagine, and even very firmly believe, that they have done in a waking state all that of which they dreamt while sleeping. [Laguna, 1555, IV, xxv, pp. 421–22]

Another example belonging here is due to Porta, a colleague of Galileo, who similarly suggested a physiological explanation of the witches' salve:

. . . although they [witches] themselves mix in a great deal of superstition, nevertheless it is apparent to the observer that these things result from a natural force. I shall repeat the things I have heard from them.

They take boys' fat and boil it in a copper vessel, then strain it; they then knead the residue. With it they mix eleoselinum, aconite [a deadly poison; see Murray, 1962: 279], poplar branches and soot. Or sometimes sium, common acorum, cinquefoil, the blood of a bat, sleep-inducing nightshade [solanum somni-ferum], and oil; and if they mix in other items, they differ somewhat from these. As soon as it is finished, they anoint the parts of the body, having rubbed them very thoroughly before, so that they grow rosy, and heat returns, and that which was stiff with cold becomes penetrable. So that the flesh may be loose and the pores open, they add, moreover, fat or, alternately, flowing oil that the force of the juices may descend inward, and be more powerful and lively. I think it not at all questionable that this is the reason.

Thus, on some moonlit night they think that they are carried off to banquets, music, dances, and coupling with young men, which they desire most of all. So great is the force of the imagination and the appearance of the images, that the part of the brain called memory is almost full of this sort of thing; and since they themselves, by inclination of nature, are extremely prone to belief, they take hold of the images in such a way that the mind itself is changed and thinks of nothing else day or night. They are strengthened in this by their eating nothing but beets, roots, chestnuts, and vegetables.

While I was working on this matter, searching out everything most diligently—for I was still in a state of ambivalent judgment—an old woman came to my notice ([one of those] whom they call screech-owls [striges], from the resemblance between the night-owl [strix] and the witches [strigae], and who suck the blood of tiny children in their cradles); who promised of her own accord to bring me answers in a short while. She ordered all of us who were gathered there with me as witnesses to go outside. Then she stripped off all her rags and rubbed herself very thoroughly and heartily with some ointment (she was visible to us through the cracks of the door). Then she sank down from the force of the soporific juices and fell into a deep sleep. We then opened the doors and gave her quite a flogging; the force of her stupor was so great that it had taken away her senses. We returned to our place outside. Then the powers of the drug grew weak and feeble and she, called from her sleep, began to babble that she had crossed seas and mountains to fetch these false answers. We denied; she insisted; we showed her the black-and-blue marks; she insisted more tenaciously than before.

What, then, shall I think of these affairs? There will be place enough to tell of other witches; let our discussion return for the moment to its proper arrangement; we have been sufficiently loquacious. This, moreover, I think should be pointed out, lest those who experiment grow discouraged: these things do not turn out the same for all people. As for example, for melancholics, since their nature is chill and cold nothing very much happens to them from the warming-up methods of the witches. . . . [Porta, 1562, II, xxvii, pp. 197–98]

Twentieth-Century Comparative Data

Shortly before the turn of the present century, a German scholar of the occult, Karl Kiesewetter ([1902?]: 579), inspired by the accounts of Porta and others, made a sample of the witches' ointment. After rubbing himself with it, he experienced a dream in which he was flying in spirals. More recently, Professor Will-Erich Peukert of Göttingen, Germany, is reported to have made a flying ointment of belladonna, henbane, and *Datura*, employing a seventeenth-century formula. According to the report he:

. . . rubbed it on his forehead and armpits and had colleagues do the same. They fell into a twenty-four hour sleep in which they dreamed of wild rides, frenzied dancing, and other weird adventures of the type connected with medieval orgies. [Krieg, 1966: 53]

Gustav Schenk has also experimented with henbane, although not in the form of an ointment. He reports that after inhaling the smoke of the burning seeds:

My teeth were clenched, and a dizzy rage took possession of me. I know that I trembled with horror; but I also know that I was permeated by a peculiar sense of well-being connected with the crazy sensation that my feet were growing lighter, expanding and breaking loose from my body. (This sensation of gradual body dissolution is typical of henbane poisoning.) Each part of my body seemed to be going off on its own. My head was growing independently larger, and I was seized with the fear that I was falling apart. At the same time I experienced an intoxicating sensation of flying.

The frightening certainty that my end was near through the dissolution of my body was counterbalanced by an animal joy in flight. I soared where my hallucinations—the clouds, the lowering sky, herds of beasts, falling leaves which were quite unlike any ordinary leaves, billowing streamers of steam and rivers of molten metal—were swirling along. [Schenk, 1955: 48]

Some years ago I ran across a reference to the use of a *Datura* ointment by the Yaqui Indians of northern Mexico, reportedly rubbed on the stomach "to see visions." I called this to the attention of my colleague and friend Carlos Castaneda, who was studying under a Yaqui shaman, and asked him to find out if the Yaqui used the ointment for flying and to determine its effects.

I quote from his subsequent experience with the ointment of *Datura*, which provides impressive evidence for its impact:

The motion of my body was slow and shaky; it was more like a tremor forward and up. I looked down and saw don Juan sitting below me, way below me. The momentum carried me forward one more step, which was even more elastic and longer than the preceding one. And from there I soared. I remember coming down once; then I pushed up with both feet, sprang backward, and glided on my back. I saw the dark sky above me, and the clouds going by me. I jerked my body so I could look down. I saw the dark mass of the mountains. My speed was extraordinary. My arms were fixed, folded against my sides. My head was the directional unit. If I kept it bent backward I made vertical circles. I changed directions by turning my head to the side. I enjoyed such freedom and swiftness as I had never known before. The marvelous darkness gave me a feeling of sadness, of longing, perhaps. It was as if I had found a place where I belonged—the darkness of night. [Castaneda, 1968: 91]

Lycanthropy

Now let us turn to lycanthropy, the belief that a human can change himself into a wolf or similar predatory animal. The possibility that hallucinogens may have been involved in such beliefs occurred to me after reading an account of a psychiatrist colleague who administered harmaline to a subject who afterwards reported that he first believed he was a bird flying through the air, then a fish, then in his own words (see Naranjo in this volume, p. 185):

> I wasn't a fish anymore, but a big cat, a tiger. I walked, though, feeling the same freedom I had experienced as a bird and a fish, freedom of movement, flexibility, grace. I moved as a tiger in the jungle, joyously, feeling the ground under my feet, feeling my power; my chest grew larger. I then approached an animal, any animal. I only saw its neck, and then experienced what a tiger feels when looking at its prey.

The neck which the subject referred to was that of a woman in the room who had appeared to him to have changed into a deer, and the subject had to be restrained from attempting to bite her neck.

This information, together with random accounts of shape changing reported by persons having LSD experiences in our culture, caused me to review the werewolf literature to see if there might be a connection with hallucinogen use.[2] The following examples illustrate some of the results.

A Greek account, by Paulus Aegineta, of lycanthropy from the fourth or seventh century A.D. is as follows (Adams, 1844: 1:389–90):

> Those labouring under lycanthropia go out during the night imitating wolves in all things and lingering about sepulchres until morning. You may recognize such persons by these marks: they are pale, their vision feeble, their eyes dry, tongue very dry, and the flow of the saliva stopped; but they are thirsty, and their legs have incurable ulcerations from frequent falls. Such are the marks of the disease.

The symptoms described closely resemble those reported for the clinical effects of atropine, specifically, dryness of the throat and mouth, difficulty in swallowing, great thirst, impaired vision, and staggering gait (Sollmann, 1957: 392). It is interesting to

2. A most useful survey of the European werewolf literature is provided by Summers (1966). While the Reverend Mr. Summers recognizes that the ointments had a role both in witchcraft and lycanthropy (p. xiv), he seems quite seriously to assign a role of at least equal importance to the "force" of the "diabolic pact" presumably made by the practitioner and to his "impious spells" (p. 123).

THE TRANSFORMATION OF WITCHES
INTO ANIMAL FORMS

Three witches in animal forms flying on a pitchfork, from a fifteenth-century woodcut

observe also that Hesse (1946: 103–4) notes: "A characteristic feature of solanaceae psychosis is furthermore that the intoxicated person imagines himself to have been changed into some animal, and the hallucinosis is completed by the sensation of the growing feathers and hair, due probably to main paraethesic."

Porta (1658 [orig. 1589]: 219) states that "To make a man believe he was changed into a Bird or Beast" a potion was drunk which was made from henbane, mandrake, stramonium or Solanum manicum, and belladonna. Under its effects, "the man would seem sometimes to be changed into a fish; and flinging out his arms, would swim on the Ground: sometimes he would seem to skip up, and then to dive down again. Another would believe himself turned into a Goose, and would eat Grass, and beat the Ground with his Teeth, like a Goose: now and then sing, and endeavor to clap his Wings."

In Goya's *Cocina de las brujas* (Witches' Kitchen), the witches are in various stages of transformation. One of the creatures, apparently a wolf, watches a cloven-hoofed beast, probably a he-goat, rise up the chimney

In a confession made before an inquisitor of the Church in 1521 in France, Pierre Bourgot admitted that he and a companion had used an ointment whose effect, when rubbed on the body, was to change them into wolves for one or two hours, and that in this state they physically attacked a number of persons on various occasions, biting them with their teeth, killing them and even eating parts of their bodies (Wier, 1885 [orig. 1660]: 263–67).

In 1599 Chauvincourt published in Paris a discourse on lycanthropy in which he concluded that such changes were illusory and produced by "unguents, powders, potions, and noxious herbs, which are able to dazzle all who come under their baleful and magic influence" (Chauvincourt, 1599).

A somewhat similar position was taken by Nynald shortly thereafter in his work, *De la lycanthropie, transformation, et extase des sorciers,* in which he also listed the ingredients of the ointments used. Among them were belladonna and henbane, as well as aconite, opium, and hashish (Nynald, 1615: ch. ii). He asserted that "all shape-shifting is mere hallucination" (Nynauld, 1615: ch. vii).

It was sometimes recorded that a girdle made of the pelt of a wolf was used in addition to the ointment. "Peter Stump, who was executed for werwolfism in 1590, confessed that the demon has bestowed a girdle upon him, with which he girt himself when the lust came upon him to shift his shape to a wolf" (Elich, 1607: 155).

Verstegan (1634: 237) reports:

> The Were-Wolues are certaine Sorcerers, who having annoynted their bodies, with an Oyntment which they make by the instinct of the Divell: And putting on a certayne Inchaunted Girdle, doe not onely unto the view of others, seeme as Wolues, but to their owne thinking have both the Shape, and Nature of Wolues, so long as they weare the sayd girdle: And they doe dispose themselues as very Wolues, in wourrying, and killing, and most of Humane Creatures.

Boguet (1929 [orig. 1602]: 150), similarly reports the use of an ointment in combination with a wolf skin:

The confessions of Jacques Boequet, Françoise Secretain, Clauda Jamquillaume, Clauda Jamprost, Thievenne Paget, Pierre Gandillon and George Gandillon are very relevant to our argument, for they said that, in order to turn themselves into wolves, they first rubbed themselves with an ointment, and then Satan clothed them in a wolf's skin which completely covered them, and that they then went on all-fours and ran about the country chasing now a person and now an animal to the guidance of their appetite.

Del Rio (1606, Liber II, quaestrio xviii, pp. 455–56) states:

At times he [the demon] fastens most closely the real skin of a beast around their [the sorcerers'] bodies: that this is done, since the wolf-skin that he furnishes is concealed in the hollow trunk of a tree, is supported by the confessions of certain witnesses.

Boguet (1929 [orig. 1602]: 151) is clearly of the view that the use of the ointment was essential to the werewolf experience:

In company with the Lord Claude Meynier, our Recorder, I have seen those I have named go on all-fours in a room just as they did when they were in the fields; but they said that it was impossible for them to turn themselves into wolves, since they had no more ointment, and they had lost the power of doing so by being imprisoned.

He also indicates that the same ointment was used both for going to the Sabbat and for becoming werewolves (Boguet, 1929 [orig. 1602]: 69): "The witches anoint themselves with it [ointment] when they go to the Sabbat, or when they change into wolves."

It appears, then, that a solanaceous plant ointment was used both in experiencing the witches' flight and the metamorphosis into werewolf. The differing results can easily be explained from what we know of modern experiences with hallucinogenic drugs. That is, the expectations and desires of the subject and the cues in his immediate environment strongly affect the nature of his experience. We can see how the use of the broomstick or other straddling device, or the use of a wolf skin or wolf skin girdle, might be, through their tactile impact on the subject, powerful suggestive devices influencing the nature of the hallucinations.

Finally, I wish to note one of the major characteristics of medieval and Renaissance witchcraft in Europe which helps distinguish it from ordinary shamanism. This is the fact that the witches performed their acts of bewitching and of mutual aid while *not* in a trance, but as part of a ritual meeting called the Esbat which has been described as a "business" meeting. This was a real gathering not connected with the use of the hallucinogenic ointment and was clearly distinguished both in name and substance from the Sabbat or Sabbath to which one flew and where one participated in orgiastic encounters with demons. In other words, unlike classical shamans, the sorcerer in Europe had his trance encounters with the spirit world on occasions distinguished from his *manipulation* of that supernatural world. I believe the reason for this major distinguishing feature of European witchcraft lies in the nature of the drugs they were using. Specifically, the solanaceous hallucinogens are so powerful that it is essentially impossible for the user to control his mind and body sufficiently to perform ritual activity at the same time. In addition, the state of extended sleep following the period of initial excitation, sleep which can extend for three or four days, together with the typical amnesia, made this hardly a convenient method for daily practice of witchcraft. Furthermore, there is some ethnographic evidence that too frequent use of the solanaceous drugs can permanently derange the mind.

I arrived at this particular insight about the problems of using solanaceous plants in shamanism and witchcraft during my fieldwork among the Jívaro Indians (*untsuri šuara*) of eastern Ecuador, who use both the solanaceous plant, *Datura*, and non-solanaceous hallucinogens. They utilize the solanaceous plant in the vision quest, simply to encounter the supernatural, but do not use it in shamanism because it is "too strong," and prevents the shaman from being able to operate in both worlds simultaneously. The European witches, in my opinion, had an entirely reasonable ritual system of using the solanaceous plants, given their great effects. Thus, the fact that traditional European witchcraft involves the separation of trance states from ritual operations may be largely due to the problems of coping with the particular hallucinogens they used. This would explain the peculiar existence of both Sabbats and Esbats in European witchcraft, and also raises the question of whether shamans have to be in a trance state at the same time that they are engaged in their manipulative activities. If not, it may be necessary to revise our conceptions of the scope of shamanism and to extend it to include some of the central aspects of witchcraft as it was formerly practiced in Europe.

REFERENCES

Adams, Francis
   1844   *The Seven Books of Paulus Aegineta.* Translated from the Greek. 3 vols. London: Sydenham Society.

Barnett, Bernard
   1965   Witchcraft, Psychopathology and Hallucinations. *British Journal of Psychiatry* 3: 439–45.

Baroja, Julio C.
   1964   *The World of the Witches.* Translated by O. N. V. Glendinning. Chicago: University of Chicago Press. Original Spanish edition, 1961.

Bergamo, Jordanes de
   c.1470–71   *Qvaestio de Strigis.* Unpublished manuscript, Bibliothèque National, Paris. Quoted in Joseph Hansen, *Quellen und Untersuchen zur Geschichte des Hexenwahns und der Hexenverfolgung im Mittelalter*, pp. 195–200. 1901 [1905]. Bonn: Carl Georgi.

Boguet, Henry
   1929   *An Examen of Witches. Drawn from various trials . . .* Translated by E. Allen Ashwin. Edited by the Rev. Montague Summers. London: John Rodker. Original French edition, 1602.

Castaneda, Carlos
   1968   *The Teachings of Don Juan: A Yaqui Way of Knowledge.* Berkeley and Los Angeles: University of California Press.

Chauvincourt, Sieur de Beauvoys de
   1599   *Discours de la lycanthropie ou de la transmutation des hommes en loups.* Paris.

Ciruelo, Pedro
   1628   *Tratado en el qual se repruevan todas la supersticiones y hechizerías.* Barcelona. Quoted in H. C. Lea, *Materials Toward a History of Witchcraft*, p. 413. 1957. New York and London: Thomas Yoseloff.

Claus, Edward P., and Varro E. Tyler
1965 *Pharmacognosy.* 5th edition. Philadelphia: Lea and Febiger.
Del Rio, Martin
1606 *Disquisitionum Magicarum Libri Sex.* Mainz.
Elich, Ludwig
1607 *Doemonomagia.* Francofurti.
Glanvil, Joseph
1681 *Saducismus Triumphatus.* London.
Henningsen, Gustav
1969 The Papers of Alonso de Salazar Frias: A Spanish Witchcraft Polemic 1610–14. *Temenos* 5: 85–106 (Turku, Fin-
land).
Henry, Thomas A.
1949 *The Plant Alkaloids.* 4th edition. London: J. and A.
Churchill.
Hesse, Erich
1946 *Narcotics and Drug Addiction.* New York: Philosophical
Library.
Hoffer, A., and H. Osmund
1967 *The Hallucinogens.* New York and London: Academic Press.
Holinshed, Raphael
1577 *The Chronicles of England, Scotlande, and Irelande.* London. Imprinted for G. Bishop.
Jones, Ernest
1931 *On the Nightmare.* London: Hogarth Press.
Kiesewetter, Karl
[1902?] *Die Geheimwissenschaften.* Zweite Auflage. Leipsig: Wil-
helm Friedrich. Foreword written 1894.
Krieg, Margaret B.
1966 *Green Medicine: The Search for Plants That Heal.* New
York: Bantam.
Laguna, Andrés
1555 *Materia Medica.* Antwerp. Quoted in Marcel Bataillon,
Contes à la Première Personne (Extraits des Livres Sérieux
du Docteur Laguna), *Bulletin Hispanique* 58: 201–6. 1956.
Lewin, Louis
1964 *Phantastica, Narcotic and Stimulating Drugs: Their Use and
Abuse.* Translated from the 2nd German edition by P. H. A.
Wirth. New York: E. P. Dutton. Original German edition,
1924.

Murray, Margaret
    1962   *The Witch-Cult in Western Europe*. London: Oxford University Press. Originally published in 1921.
Nider, Johannes
    1692   *Formicarivs. Helmstädt*.
Nynald, Sieur Jean de
    1615   *De la lycanthropie, transformation, et extase des sorciers*. Paris.
Porta, Giovanni Battista [John Baptista Porta]
    1562   *Magiae Naturalis, siue de Miraculis Rerum Naturalium Libri IIII*. Cologne.
    1658   *Natural Magick*. Translated from the expurgated Italian edition of 1589. Reproduction of the 1658 English edition. New York: Basic Books. 1957.
Remy, Nicolas [Nicholas Remigius, Nic. Remigii]
    1596   *Daemonolatreia Libri Tres*. Cologne.
Schenk, Gustav
    1955   *The Book of Poisons*. Translated from the German by Michael Bullock. New York: Rinehart.
Sollmann, Torald
    1957   *A Manual of Pharmacology and Its Applications to Therapeutics and Toxicology*. 8th edition. Philadelphia and London: W. B. Saunders.
Spina, Bartolommeo
    1523   *Qvaestio de Strigibvs*. Venice.
Summers, Montague
    1966   *The Werewolf*. New Hyde Park, N. Y.: University Books.
Trevor-Roper, H. R.
    1969   *The European Witch-Craze of the Sixteenth and Seventeenth Centuries and Other Essays*. New York and Evanston: Harper and Row.
Tylor, Edward B.
    1924   *Primitive Culture: Researches into the Development of Mythology, Philosophy, Religion, Language, Art, and Custom*. 2 vols. (combined). New York: Brentano's. Originally published 1871.
Verstegan, Richard
    1637   *A Restitution of Decayed Intelligence: In Antiquities Concerning the Most Noble, and Renowned English Nation*. London: John Norton.

Vincent, Johann
   c.1475   *Liber Adversvs Magicas Artes*. Inedited manuscript, Biblio-
            thèque National, Paris. Quoted *in* Joseph Hansen, *Quellen
            und Untersuchen zur Geschichte des Hexenwahns und der
            Hexenverfolgung im Mittelalter*, pp. 227–31. 1901 [1905].
            Bonn: Carl Georgi.
Wier, Jean
   1885   *Histoires, dispvtes et discovrs*. Vol. II. Paris: Bureau du
            Progrès Médical. Originally published 1660.

IV

Hallucinogens and Shamanism: The Question of a Trans-Cultural Experience

WHILE the preceding articles have largely tended to focus on the particular sociocultural contexts of hallucinogen use in connection with shamanism in specific cultures, the reader has probably noticed the recurrence of certain themes of belief or experience as, for example, the shamanistic journey or flight. Normally the anthropologist simply views such widespread and obviously long-standing thematic regularities as part of the totality of the ancient cultural heritage of man, and does not usually attempt to explain their existence. Attempts at explanation for such phenomena, commonly viewed as the search for "origins," have tended to fall into disrepute as an antiquated kind of anthropology associated with such nineteenth-century figures as the English anthropologist Edward B. Tylor. There is some justification for this attitude in that explanations of ancient "origins" can hardly be proven one way or another and do not seem relevant to understanding why a particular belief or practice is present in a culture being studied now. However, if one redefines the search for origins as the search for causality of regularities, the quest assumes great importance for the study of all human cultures, past and present.

Culture is learned and transmitted through human effort; therefore it seems unlikely that cultural institutions and traits can be successfully passed on through centuries and millennia without having some regular reinforcement for their maintenance. Thus when we find some obviously ancient and widely distributed belief such as the shamanistic journey, it seems logical to wonder whether there might not be some generalized biochemical reinforcement for the belief that is not dependent upon the particularistic details of the cultures in which it is found.

A peculiar confirmation of the thesis of a non-cultural origin and continuing basis for some of these beliefs is the independent invention of the concept of the "trip" in the United States during the early 1960's to describe the nature of the hallucinogenic drug experience. Even the more specific contemporary concept, "to have a good trip," has its precise linguistic parallel among the Cashinahua of the Amazon rain forest, as reported by Kensinger in this volume. Thanks to the effects of the Inquisition in eradicating much of the ideology of European witchcraft, the return of the concept of the hallucinogenically induced journey, trip, or flight to modern Western culture cannot be easily ascribed to cultural tradition.

While it is fairly understandable that a biochemical change in the human nervous system may be responsible for the widespread belief in the shamanistic journey, there remain subtler and even more intriguing questions as to the relationship of hallucinatory experiences to the actual content of shamanistic and religious ideology, as was long ago suggested by Tylor (1924 [orig. 1871], Vol. 1: 445–46, 450; Vol. 2: 416–19). This is not to suggest that culture-specific factors are not significant; indeed the evidence is that they are of overwhelming importance in influencing both the content and structure of supernatural ideology. Sociologists and anthropologists, following Durkheim (e.g., 1965 [orig. 1912]) and others, have long since carried the day in demonstrating their significance. There is, however, a residue that remains, which cannot be conveniently explained away by recourse to the social structure or content of particular cultures. The two papers following, by Naranjo and myself, are intended to help stimulate thought and research into the question of the degree to which biochemical changes, whether or not induced by hallucinogens, may underlie regularities in the content of "otherworldly" experiences and especially widespread and long-persisting fundamental themes in human belief.

In these companion papers, meant to be read as a unit, the experiences of two culturally distinct populations are outlined in terms of their subjective reactions following ingestion of the *Banisteriopsis* drink or one of its major hallucinogenic alkaloids. Harner surveys the reports of visions by South American tropical forest Indians, particularly in the Amazon, while Naranjo describes the experiences of white urban Chileans with the same drink or with harmaline, one of its chief chemical components (see Hoffer and Osmund, 1967: 478–80), under clinical conditions. Naranjo's subjects were unaware of the source of the substance administered to them, or its connection with Amazon Indians, or of its expected effects. His subjects reported experiences which repeat well-known themes of the shamanistic experience, including: the sensation of a soul separate or distinct from the body; flight; metamorphosis into a mammal, bird, or fish; and spirit possession. In addition, the white urban Chilean subjects not infrequently saw two of the main kinds of visions specific to the experience of the tropical forest Indians using the drug: reptiles and large felines. In the Indians' case, the felines were characteristically jaguars; in the Chilean study, the felines were tigers, leopards, and jaguars. Birds of prey were also seen. This result was unexpected and remains unexplained. A possible psychoanalytic explanation of such visions of predatory animals might be that they are oral aggressive phenomena brought to consciousness in some individuals as they regress under the influence of the drug. Alternatively, in view of the probability that the chief predators on man's small primate ancestors included large felines, crocodiles, serpents, and birds of prey, it would be tempting to speculate as to whether there might exist genetically-based fear cues or images which have been biochemically stimulated by the *yagé* alkaloids and which might once have had a positive adaptive value in terms of natural selection.

However, serious consideration of any explanatory hypotheses must await the collection of better data derived from rigorous comparative, experimental, and cross-cultural research involving not only anthropology but psychology and related disciplines.

9

Common Themes in South American Indian Yagé Experiences[1]

Michael J. Harner

The existence of a hallucinatory drink made from the South American tropical forest *ayahuasca* or *yagé* vine (*Banisteriopsis*) was perhaps first reported to the Western world by the Ecuadorian geographer, Villavicencio. He observed (1858: 372–73):

> . . . this beverage is narcotic, as one might suppose, and in a few moments it begins to produce the most rare phenomena. Its action appears to excite the nervous system; all the senses liven up and all faculties awaken; they feel vertigo and spinning in the head, then a sensation of being lifted into the air and

1. The data on Jívaro and Conibo-Shipibo Indian experiences are derived from fieldwork by the author among the former in 1956–57 and 1964; and among the latter in 1960–61.

In 1961, while engaged in ethnographic fieldwork among the Conibo Indians of eastern Peru, I partook of *ayahuasca* to try to understand the nature of the personal revelations occurring to these people under its influence. So impressive were the effects of the drug that a number of questions were raised in my mind as to the cross-cultural importance of the hallucinogenic experience in shamanism and religion. One result is the present paper and the one which follows by Claudio Naranjo which are intended to be read in conjunction with one another, and which were presented in an earlier form at the annual meeting of the American Anthropological Association at Denver in 1965. This paper, written prior to the descriptions of *Banisteriopsis* use and experiences contributed by other anthropologists to this volume, does not embody their data. I wish to express my appreciation to Dale Valory for research assistance.

beginning an aerial journey; the possessed begins in the first moments to see the most delicious apparitions, in conformity with his ideas and knowledge: the savages [apparently the Záparo of eastern Ecuador] say that they see gorgeous lakes, forests covered with fruit, the prettiest birds who communicate to them the nicest and the most favorable things they want to hear, and other beautiful things relating to their savage life. When this instant passes they begin to see terrible horrors out to devour them, their first flight ceases and they descend to earth to combat the terrors who communicate to them all adversities and misfortunes awaiting them.

As for myself I can say for a fact that when I've taken *ayahuasca* I've experienced dizziness, then an aerial journey in which I recall perceiving the most gorgeous views, great cities, lofty towers, beautiful parks, and other extremely attractive objects; then I imagined myself to be alone in a forest and assaulted by a number of terrible beings from which I defended myself; thereafter I had the strong sensation of sleep. . . .

Despite this early and intriguing report, subsequent ethnographic research into the use and effects of this hallucinogen has until recently been surprisingly limited. More specifically, ethnographic reports on South American Indian accounts of their experiences resulting from the ingestion of *yagé* or *ayahuasca* brews of *Banisteriopsis* are scattered and typically lacking in adequate detail. Yet regularities are discernible, and some of the more commonly reported ones will be noted in the following pages.[2] General observations on the *ayahuasca* experience have been made by Villarejo (1953: 190–91):

Shortly after having drunk the potion, a hyper-excitation is felt in the body, which produces a pleasant agitation in the epiderm and livens the kinesthetic sense, giving one the imagined state of being suspended in air. Once the narcotic is fully activated, various mental reactions and activities, or merely phantasmagoric, supervene.

One under the control of the narcotic sees unroll before him quite a spectacle: most lovely landscapes, monstrous animals, vipers which approach and wind down his body or are entwined

2. For information on the botanical and pharmacological aspects of *Banisteriopsis* drinks, see pages 1–5.

like rolls of thick cable, at a few centimeters distance; as well, one sees who are true friends and those who betray him or who have done him ill; he observes the cause of the illness which he sustains, at the same time being presented with the most advantageous remedy; he takes part in fantastic hunts; the things which he most dearly loves or abhors acquire in these moments extraordinary vividness and color, and the scenes in which his life normally develop adopt the most beautiful and emotional expression.

Supplementary information on the effects of the brew are provided by Reinburg (1921: 28–29), one of the very few anthropologists to partake of the drink. In his diary he noted:

Comprehension is highly exaggerated; it seems to me as though my body has disappeared; I am nothing more than a mind observing with interest the phases of experience going on within another person.

My pulse is *extremely* slackened, but I do not know how many pulses it is beating; blood pressure is greatly diminished, at least it seems to be to my touch; then my pulse returns at instances, imperceptibly, and the nausea increases. Not feeling well, I inform Teofilo who reassures me, saying that that's just perfect, that the beneficial (!) effect of the *ayahuasca* is beginning and that I am going to see visions.

Not very reassured, in the meantime, I have the lamp lit and ask for a mirror: I am livid, my pupils dilated do not react to the light, my hands have shaky movements, abrupt and rapid as though I was trying to seize something. The earache has increased, but hearing is perfect; the nausea increases and becomes very unpleasant; and, abandoning the precepts of *ayahuasca* drinkers who desire to let the phenomena thereof amend themselves, I try forcibly to vomit and take tea, especially because my heart bothers me. I get up (midnight), urinate profusely, having difficulty holding myself upright, and make the two or three steps which separate me from my room, where I try to light the chafing-dish in order to prepare the tea. But there, I am taken by a weakness and fall in a heap upon a bottle-case, crying to Teofilo, "I've been poisoned." My pulse has completely disappeared, I am livid, my pupils dilated, the throat locked with a strong dysphagia, dryness in my mouth, the sensation of the lower part of my body disappearing, uncontrollable movements of the hands in attempting to pick up anything; extremely accentuated thymus, speech very difficult and erratic.

Reinburg's experience was interrupted by the administration of stimulants, and he never did achieve visions, but his physical symptoms remarkably parallel those which I experienced without previous knowledge of Reinburg's account. In my case, visions, sounds, singing, and other hallucinatory material were plentiful, with the first effects (numbness in the jaw) occurring within fifteen minutes and actual visionary material within five minutes after that. The period of immersion in visions lasted about three hours in its deepest effect, with an additional hour of tapering off.

I will not dwell further on the experiences of Reinburg, myself, and other whites who have taken the drug in the jungle. The companion paper by Claudio Naranjo deals with such experiences in a situation more controlled for comparative purposes. Let us turn to some common denominators which can be observed in the reported experiences of Indians of the tropical forest who take the drug as part of their normal cultural life. A survey of the literature reveals the following to be among the most commonly reported hallucinatory experiences:

1. The Soul Is Believed to Separate from the Physical Body and to Make a Trip, Often with the Sensation of Flight

Among the Jívaro, it is felt that part of the soul may leave the body, with the subject having the sensation of flying, returning when the effects of the drug wear off. This is actually referred to as a "trip" by the Jívaro, who say that this is an experience more commonly achieved by shamans than by other takers of the brew.

The Conibo-Shipibo Indians of the Ucayali region of eastern Peru report that a common function of ayahuasca-taking by shamans is to permit the shaman's soul to leave his body in the form of a bird which flies to kill a distant person at night. The bird changes back into the shaman's human form to kill the sleeping person. Another typical experience of Conibo-Shipibo shamans is setting out in a supernatural launch manned by demons to recapture the stolen soul of a sick patient from the demon launch of an enemy shaman. A non-shaman under the influence of *aya-huasca* may likewise have his soul taken away by a demon launch. Under such circumstances, his body appears to observers as "dead," with no noticeable heart beat nor respiration, according to the Indians. A shaman, taking *ayahuasca*, pursues and recovers the patient's soul.

Among the Amahuaca, eastern neighbors of the Conibo in the Peruvian Montaña, it is reported by the Indians that "a man's soul may leave his body when he drinks *ayahuasca*" (Carneiro, n.d.).

For the Záparo of eastern Ecuador, as noted before, Villavicencio (1858: 372) reports: "they feel vertigo and spinning in the head, then a sensation of being lifted into the air and begin an aerial journey."

Of the group *yagé* session of the Desana branch of the Tukano Indians in eastern Colombia, Reichel-Dolmatoff (1971: 173) reports:

> The hallucination has several phases, and during the first the person feels and hears a violent current of air, as if a strong wind were pulling him along; the *kumú* [ritual leader] explains that it is the ascent to the Milky Way; in order to arrive at their final destination, they must leave this world and first find the current of communication with the winds. Now, following the Milky Way, the men descend to *Ahpikondiá* [Paradise].

Among the Siona of the Putumayo region of Colombia, Plácido de Calella (1944: 745) reports of the man apprenticed to become a shaman and taking *yagé*: "In this state he goes off to heaven (the sky) several times, with God (Diosú), where he spends one night and descends again." The accomplished shaman leads group sessions, makes trips to heaven to learn God's wishes, returns to reveal them to the group, and also makes trips to Hell. "It is necessary for one to be a very good *curaca* [shaman-leader] or drinker in order to be able to penetrate to the deepest of Hell, because one is jeopardized such that he might not know how to get out of there and might have to remain" (Plácido de Calella, 1944: 747).

A half-breed Peruvian woman, in the Río Guaporé region near the Brazil-Bolivia frontier, whose family used *ayahuasca* regularly, told E. H. Snethlage in 1933–34 that the drug freed the spirit which was then "able to travel where it desired" (Santesson and Wassén, 1936: 341).

In describing the effects of *ayahuasca*, apparently on both Indians and whites in the upper Amazon, Villarejo (1953: 190) says that it puts the drinker into "the imagined state of being suspended in the air" shortly after taking the hallucinatory concoction.

Chaves (1958: 131) reports on some specific experiences under the influence of *yagé* recounted by a Siona Indian of eastern Colombia:

> But then an aging woman came to wrap me in a great cloth, gave me to suckle at her breast, and then off I flew, very far, and suddenly I found myself in a completely illumined place, very clear, where everything was placid and serene. There, where the *yagé* people live, like us, but better, is where one ends up [i.e., on a *yagé* "trip"].

Grandidier (1861: 143) states that among the Campa Indians of eastern Peru a sick person may take *ayahuasca* ("*camalampi*" in Campa) with the result that ". . . he is drunk, his head spins, he thinks he is flying through the air, he is prey to strange apparitions. . . ."

Oberem (1958: 80) says that among the long-missionized Quijos Indians of the Río Napo of eastern Ecuador two *ayahuasca*-using shamans told him that they "have the power to go to a place beneath the earth, beneath Hell, from which they are able to bewitch somebody."

2. *Visions of Snakes and Jaguars*

The visions most commonly reported for all tribes are of snakes, generally poisonous varieties and the anaconda, and of jaguars and other dangerous forest felines. In some cases, these predatory creatures appear to threaten or attack the *yagé*-taker.

Among the Jívaro, the most typical apparitions seen on the vision quest by persons taking the *Banisteriopsis* drink or *Datura* are pairs of giant anacondas or jaguars which roll over and over through the forest as they fight between themselves (see Harner,

1962: 260–61, 271) (see Fig. I). The shamans under the influence of *ayahuasca*, see snakes apparently at least as often as any other single class of beings (see Fig. II). Sometimes they also see caymans (Fig. III). The intruding objects to be sucked out of the patient's body very commonly have the appearance of various snakes to the shaman (see Fig. IV).

I. Jaguar drawn by a Jívaro shaman after a *Datura* trance. Jaguars are often seen in fighting pairs in the trances; in this instance the artist recalled only one

Villavicencio (1858: 372), in his early account of *yagé* experiences among the Záparo of eastern Ecuador, does not mention specific predatory animals as appearing in the visions, but does say "they begin to see terrible horrors out to devour them."

Pérez Arbélaez (1937: 175) reports that some Coreguajes Indians from San Miguel, Colombia, when asked what one of their *curacas* saw when he took *yagé*, replied that he saw "all kinds of boars [*puercos*], tapirs, and jaguars [*tigres*] out in the forest."

Carneiro (1964: 9) reports for the Amahuaca Indians of Peru:

Taking *ayahuasca* for the first time is apparently a rather frightening experience for a young man. Some of them reported seeing snakes crawling up their bodies. The *yoshi* [spirit] of the jaguar is the one most often seen at this time, and it teaches the apprentice drinkers all about *yoshi*.

Also (Carneiro, 1964: 10):

> The most important *yoshi* connected with witchcraft is that of the jaguar. This *yoshi* appears to the sorcerer after he has drunk *ayahuasca* and tells him everything he wants to know, including the whereabouts of the intended victim.

For the Cubeo of the Colombian Amazon, Goldman (1963: 210) reports:

> At the beginning, the Indians say, the vision becomes blurred, things begin to look white, and one begins to lose the faculty of speech. The white vision turns to red. One Indian described it as a room spinning with red feathers. This passes and one begins to see people in the bright coloring of the jaguar.

Describing the *yagé* experiences of the Tukano Indians of eastern Colombia, Reichel-Dolmatoff (1969: 335) reports:

> Occasionally the individual wakes from his trance in a state of great calm and profound satisfaction; other times he may hardly be able to grasp partial visions, fleeting and disturbing images difficult to interpret. And on still other occasions the person remains overwhelmed by the nightmare of jaguars' jaws or the menace of snakes that approach while he, paralyzed by fear, feels how their cold bodies go coiling around his extremities.

Speaking of the Desana group of the Tukano, he (Reichel-Dolmatoff, 1969: 332–33) also notes:

> A certain *yajé* belonging to the Desana makes one see "feather crowns that jump" or snakes in the form of necklaces that coil around the houseposts. Another kind of *yajé* is said to produce hallucinations of "snakes that jump."

Koch-Grünberg (1909: 190), in a chapter on the Tukano and Desana Indians, similarly says that the Indians see "brightly-colored snakes winding up and down the house-posts."

Chaves (1958: 134) reports that among the Siona of the upper Putumayo River in Colombia:

> When the drinker of *yagé* is a novice, he sees serpents, tigers, and other nonsense. These snakes represent the vines of the *yagé*; at times many snakes are seen in one bunch and one can-

not escape from them. For this reason, he who conquers *yagé* also conquers nature and all the dangers which attack men. Thus the Siona explain the taking of *yagé*.

A Siona informant described his first *yagé* experience as follows (Mallol de Recasens, 1963: 65):

> After drinking the *yagé*, I went to lie down in a hammock; shortly I began to see small snakes in great quantity, then a large snake in a shrub which, when it shook, dropped something like scales.

For the Piro of eastern Peru, Baer (1969: 6) states that an informant reported that under the influence of *ayahuasca*:

> . . . he had seen a great boa constrictor in his trance, that he had become afraid and had attempted to keep the boa away or to fend it off with his hands. In the attempt to take hold of it, he had recognized that no boa was there.

Tessmann (1930: 517) says that among the Ikito (Iquito) Indians of northeastern Peru:

> Enough of the drink is taken so that one collapses. Thereafter an alien substance takes possession. Even though one may see many animals, for example jaguars and great serpents rushing about, one is to have no feelings of fear.

Zerba-Bayon states (Fabre, 1955: 50) that the Indians in the Caquetá region, after taking *yagé*, "always end up being seized by a mad delirium; believing themselves to have been taken by ferocious beasts, they plunge into the forests in order to imitate their howling and break to pieces everything they find in their path . . ."

Santesson and Wassén (1936: 341) report that the previously mentioned half-breed woman interviewed by Snethlage in Bolivia said that her people took a drink made from *Banisteriopsis* and known locally as "huascar" [*ayahuasca?*] and "when properly drunk they had visions of animals, particularly snakes . . ."

Under the influence of the *Banisteriopsis* drink, the Conibo-Shipibo Indians of the Ucayali River region in eastern Peru commonly see giant anacondas, poisonous snakes, and jaguars, and, less frequently, other animals. The novice shaman, taking the drink, believes he acquires giant snakes which are to be his personal demons to be used in defending himself against other shamans in supernatural battles. The Conibo-Shipibo shamans, under the influence of the drug, believe they capture and recover other persons' souls with supernatural boats whose demon crews are led by a yellow jaguar and a black puma.

Among the Yekuaná Indians of southern Venezuela, Koch-Grünberg (1917: 324) reports that under the influence of *caapi* the shamans mimic the roars of jaguars. He does not, unfortunately, describe the contents of Yekuaná Indians' experiences under the influence of the brew.

Joy and Schultes (1955: 127) report that when the Taiwano Indians of the Kananari River of eastern Colombia drink *yagé*:

> There can be no question that they see jaguars and other animals, but the hallucinations come in a semi-dream state and usually are not frightening to them.

Villarejo (1953: 191) states that among the Indians of the upper Napo River (tribe unspecified), *ayahuasca*, when brewed with the addition of a plant called *amarón-yagé* (literally, boa-*yagé*), produces visions of boa constrictors "of all sizes which approach menacingly, and crawl down the body leaving the sensation of their weight, their stench, and their clammy character. When the hallucinating person becomes frightened and cries out in fear, the *ayahuasquero* (the man administering the *ayahuasca*) fans him with the leaves of the '*huasca huayra china panga*,' while saying: 'Be off, snake. Hasten, get thee away from here, boa.' With this act the vision disappears. The hallucinating person can continue experiencing one or another vision according to his will."

Villarejo (1953: 190) apparently is generalizing about the effects of *ayahuasca* on both Indians and whites on the upper Amazon when he states that a person under its influence sees "snakes which approach and wind down his body or are entwined like rolls of thick cables at a few centimeters distance . . ."

Use of *ayahuasca* among the Ixiamas Chama (Tacana) Indians of tropical forest Bolivia produces, according to Hissink (1960: 524), "hallucinations which involve the approach of beasts, especially jaguars and serpents of supernaturally great size."

Reinburg (1921:31) states of the Záparo of eastern Ecuador, among whom he worked, who take either *"ayahuasca* alone, or with *yagé* added," that "their principal apparitions are the jaguar [*tigre*], snake, the enemies of neighboring tribes (Jívaro mostly, and Tukano) or the animals that they meet while hunting during their rounds in the forest: different birds, monkeys, tapirs, deer, etc. . . ."

Chaves (1958: 131–32) describes the visions reported by a Siona Indian during his apprenticeship as a boy. Of the nine visions described, two involve snakes and one refers to jaguar "paintings":

(1) "When he gave me the third drink of *yagé,* I saw numerous snakes which came out of bonfires in incalculable numbers. . . ."

(2) "I went into a very beautiful house, all the people came out adorned with feathers and rattles [strings of beads from dried fruits with which the Siona adorn themselves] and they all attended to my getting dressed in this manner as well. The ponchos [*kusmas*] that they wore had paintings of jaguars [*tigres*] and various designs."

(3) "Then I went through the water to the place where the anaconda is found, who is the mistress and mother of fish; she has the form of a woman, and lives in a big house in the water where all the fish are born."

3. *Hallucinations Interpreted by the Indians as Visions of Demons and/or Deities*

A sense of experiencing first-hand contact with the supernatural seems to become almost routine with the aid of the *Banisteriopsis* drink. Thus Carneiro (1964:9), reporting upon group *ayahuasca* sessions among the Amahuaca, can note as an apparently commonplace occurrence that:

As the drug takes effect, *yoshi* [spirits] begin to appear, one or two at a time. They are said to drink *ayahuasca,* too, and to sing along with the men. The Amahuaca ask a *yoshi* where he has been and what he has seen, and he tells them. Unlike dreams, in which *yoshi* occasionally molest or injure a person, in *ayahuasca* séances they are generally friendly and tractable. It is just like when Amahuaca came to visit, we were told. A *yoshi* may stay an hour or two, and then he goes. But then another one comes, drinks with the Amahuaca, talks with them, and then he too departs. In this manner many *yoshi* may be seen and interrogated during the course of the night.

Regarding the Desana group of the Tukano in eastern Colombia, Reichel-Dolmatoff (1971: 174) says:

> On awakening from the trance, the individual remains convinced of the truth of the religious teachings. He has seen everything; he has seen V*aí-mahsë* [Master of Game Animals] and the Daughter of the Sun, he has heard her voice; he has seen the Snake-Canoe float through the rivers, and he has seen the first men spring from it. The voice of the kumú [ritual leader] has guided him and has explained everything to him in detail.

The visions also strengthen the belief in the reality of witchcraft, as is illustrated in the accompanying drawings made by a Jívaro shaman (see Figs. IV, V).

Carneiro (n.d.) was told by an Amahuaca informant that "one can get the *yoshi* to help him by drinking *ayahuasca*, and talking to *yoshi*." Also that a shaman (*hawa'ai*) "can order a *yoshi* to go and kill somebody" but "he has to first drink *ayahuasca* before he can get communication with *yoshi*, however."

Among the Quijo Indians of eastern Ecuador, Oberem (1958: 78) notes that the shaman in this group, as among the Jívaro immediately to the south, is able to see the magical darts which other shamans throw at him in order to cause illness and death:

> If the *sagra* is strong he catches them and puts them at his side on the ground and, since they hurt him a great deal, he asks the lightning to come down from the heavens to destroy these "darts" [demons].

> During the delirium, whenever a "dart" appears in his imagination, lightning flashes when the latter is approaching, during which time he defends himself with a mat of *huairashina panga* leaves, and it (the lightning) dispatches it with a blast.

The Conibo Indians of eastern Peru similarly believe that the taking of *ayahuasca* permits them to see the supernatural aspect of nature. They believe that only the man taking *ayahuasca* can see the demons in the air, including demons who act as doctors, and that, when the demon doctors come and sing, only the shaman taking *ayahuasca* is able to hear them and thus join them in singing. One Conibo shaman said that the demon doctor he sees when taking *ayahuasca* is a white man arriving in an airplane, launch, or on a bicycle (these are familiar to the Conibo from visits to Peruvian settlements). After this particular kind of demon doctor leaves, the shaman usually sees an Indian demon (*chai koino*) who enters the patient's body to suck out the intruding object causing the illness.

The tendency of individuals to believe they are seeing the supernatural is also illustrated by Chaves' report of a Siona's visions in eastern Colombia (1958: 132). Chaves' informant, an Indian of a tribe with a history of exposure to Christianity, included among his visions the following:

> Here's another vision. I then saw God who had a big cross and blessed me.
>
> Here's another vision. Afterwards I saw a big, beautiful church and I went into it in order to see the ceremony whereby one ought to rule his people; they gave me a kind of wine, of sugary water which represents the relieving remedies which the *kuraka* gives to sick people.
>
> Here's another vision. As well I observed there a big ceibo tree where all the people that live here on earth are to be found; they are in the form of birds of various kinds. From that place I could make out a big ship and in the prow a great mirror in which could be seen countless parrots; they are the sun people. Also women of the dry season dressed in red can be seen and women of the wet season, dressed in dark, blue clothing. There all things are seen as God created them; when he wishes to punish he sends the continual winter in the form of a flood. Also from there I was capable of making out the ship of the devils, from which the evil spirits come forth who come to the earth so that people perish.

Another student of the Siona, Plácido de Calella (1944: 747), provides additional information on the sense of the supernatural contact among these missionized Indians. An informant told him:

The *Curaca*, in these sessions, goes up to heaven, asks permission to enter; they give him a very attractive new garb and introduce him into the presence of *Diosú*; but he cannot get very close to him; he speaks to him from a distance. And *Diosú* manifests to him his will, his wishes, and what he ought to tell the people. He also makes visits to Hell. *Supaí*, the *uattí* or principal demon, lets him see everything.

Another Siona Indian told Plácido de Calella (1944: 748):

The *yagé* house is like the church; in it one is to act with much reverence. At times the *curaca* warns us: *"Diosú raijí* [God is coming]." Then the people kneel and *Diosú* sprinkles all present with water. And the Indians feel the water falling on their heads. The *curaca* says: "we the Indians have our custom (or religion). *Diosú* has given us *yagé*. The same, when he was among us drank it and left it for the Indians." And drinking *yagé* the *curaca* at times lets the book of *Diosú* be seen, very pretty and his cup as well. He prays or speaks with him.

4. The Sensation of Seeing Distant Persons, "Cities," and Landscapes, Typically Interpreted by the Indians as Visions of Distant Reality, i.e., as Clairvoyance

The Jívaro shamans, under the influence of *ayahuasca*, often believe that they are seeing distant persons and what they are doing. Non-shamans frequently employ a shaman to "look" and tell them what is the current situation of distant relatives or sweethearts. These distant persons apparently have to be individuals with whom the shaman is already acquainted, so that he can "know whom to look for." Also it is normally necessary for the shaman to be already acquainted with the distant locale and the route to get there, and preferably he should know the appearance and location of the house of the person being sought. The *ayahuasca*-taker, whether shaman or non-shaman, frequently also has the experience of traveling to distant and unfamiliar villages, towns and cities of the whites which they cannot identify but whose reality is unquestioned (see Fig. VI).

The shamans of the Conibo-Shipibo tribes of eastern Peru, with the aid of *ayahuasca*, commonly have the experience of traveling underground in supernatural boats to see distant cities of the demons. These, too, are believed to be underground, but are said to be visible "because the sunlight passes through the earth."

Among the Coreguajes Indians of eastern Colombia, Pérez Arbélaez (1937: 175) reports the belief of a *yagé*-using shaman that he could travel to distant places. Of his third experience with *yagé*, a Siona Indian of eastern Colombia said (Mallol de Recasens, 1963: 67), "I saw mountainous forests, stands of ferns and the face of the Devil."

According to Roessner (1946: 14), the members of an unidentified tribe in the Ucayali River region of eastern Peru:

> . . . who frequently practice the use of *ayahuasca* sit at times together, and, drinking it, propose that they all see something of the same subject, for example: "Let's see cities!" It so happens that Indians have asked white men what those strange things (*aparatos*) are which run so swiftly along the street: they had seen automobiles, which, of course, they were not acquainted with.

Villarejo (1953: 191) states that the Indians of the upper Napo River in eastern Ecuador, taking *yagé*, see "forests, cities, wild beasts, mists . . ."

The use of *ayahuasca* by the Amahuaca shaman of eastern Peru permits him, according to Carneiro (1964: 10) to contact the jaguar spirit which "tells him everything he wants to know, including the immediate whereabouts of the intended victim [of witchcraft]."

Calderón (1944: 87) reports that the Indians of eastern Colombia, apparently the Coreguajes, use *yagé* in order to "point out places where game is abundant."

5. A Divinatory Experience, Specifically the Sensation of Seeing the Enactment of Recent Unsolved Crimes, Particularly Homicide and Theft, or of Seeing the Shaman Responsible for Bewitching a Sick or Dying Person.

Ayahuasca is utilized by curing shamans among the Jívaro of eastern Ecuador for divinatory purposes to "see" the shaman who

II. Boa constrictor

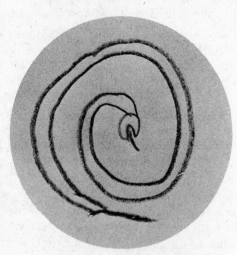

IV. Coiled snake as seen in a patient's abdomen

III. Cayman

bewitched his patient. Generally, he can recognize who it is, unless it is a shaman who lives far away, or in another tribe.

Among the Candoshi (Murato and Shapra), Tessmann (1930: 285) reports that the *caapi* drink is used "for better 'vision,' i.e., in order to discover the cause of death and then to recognize the perpetrator." He (1930: 402) similarly reports that among the Tschamikuro, "the caapi drink serves to allow one better 'vision' while curing . . ." For the Záparo, he (1930: 539) notes the use of the *caapi* drink "to allow for better diagnosing."

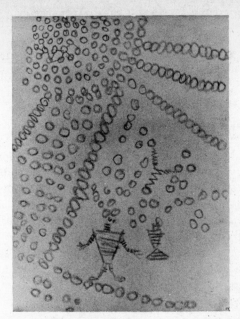

V. Golden spheres revolve about the shaman; to his left is a giant butterfly demon. The swirling field of spheres is the "spirit of *natemä*"

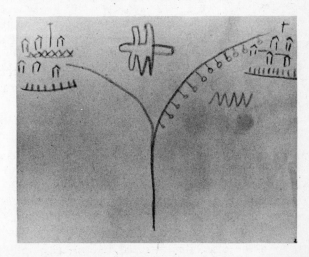

VI. A "trip." The forked lines represent the two different routes the shaman took to two white men's towns (indicated by crosses). He found one of the trails beautifully decorated with beads (shown as pendant circles)

Reichel-Dolmatoff (1960: 131–32) reports the use among the Noanamá and Emberá of the Chocó region of both *Banisteriopsis* and *Datura* "to produce hallucinations, generally with divining as the purpose." He states, without distinguishing between the effects of the two plants, that they are used "in order to identify personal enemies who seek to cause harm by their magical practices; in order to get in touch with ancestral spirits or the spirits of the animals of prey; to locate the resting place of lost or stolen articles. The visions are usually accompanied by auditory sensations and a state of euphoria they say lasts a number of hours. One of our informants, who had in past times taken *dapa* (native term for *Banisteriopsis*), described the experience thusly: 'Where there's a hill, it's whisked away; where there's water a beach is seen. All sorts of animals and people and towns are seen and all sorts of music are heard, like flutes, whistles, and drums.' "

Spruce (1908: 423–24) reports that at the Záparo village of Puca-yacu in eastern Ecuador he was told:

> If he be a medicine-man who has taken it, when he has slept off the fumes he recalls all he saw in his trance, and thereupon deduces the prophecy, divination, or what not required of him.

He also notes that the shamans of the "Záparos, Anguteros, Mazanes, and other tribes" drink *ayahuasca* "when called on to adjudicate in a dispute or quarrel—to give the proper answer to an embassy—to discover plans of an enemy—to tell if strangers are coming—to ascertain if wives are unfaithful—in the case of a sick man to tell who has bewitched him, etc."

In summary, the meager and dispersed data on the *Banisteriopsis* drink experience of tropical forest Indians tend to represent the following themes:

(1) The soul is felt to separate from the physical body and to make a trip, often with the sensation of flight.

(2) Visions of jaguars and snakes, and to a much lesser extent, other predatory animals.

(3) A sense of contact with the supernatural, whether with demons, or in the case of missionized Indians, also with God, and Heaven and Hell.

(4) Visions of distant persons, "cities" and landscapes, typi-

cally interpreted by the Indians as visions of distant reality, i.e., as clairvoyance.

(5) The sensation of seeing the detailed enactment of recent unsolved crimes, particularly homicide and theft, i.e., the experience of believing one is capable of divination.

Other experiences which are commonly reported by the Indians include auditory hallucinations and visions of geometric designs, auras, one's own death, and combats between demons or zoomorphic forms. In addition, the visions seem to involve very bright colors, and the constant changing of shapes as scenes dissolve one into another. Both Jívaro and Conibo-Shipibo Indians who had seen motion pictures told me that the *ayahuasca* experiences were comparable to the viewing of films, and my own experience was corroboratory.

In conclusion, one may note that regularities are found in *Banisteriopsis* drink experiences between tribes as widespread as the Chocó Indians west of the Andes in Colombia and the Tacana Indians east of the Andes in Bolivia. However, all of these *Banisteriopsis*-using peoples occupy a tropical forest environment and their cultures often share much in content. Given the relative contiguity as well as the environmental and cultural similarities of these tribes, it seems virtually impossible to isolate the nature of the *yagé*-induced experience from its cultural context on the basis of these ethnographic data alone. Comparative material, such as the following paper by Naranjo, may eventually help contribute to a gradual solution of this problem.

REFERENCES

Baer, Gerhard
    1969   Eine Ayahuasca-Sitzung unter den Piro (Ostperu). *Bulletin de la Société suisse des Américanistes* 33: 5–8.
Calderón, Daniel
    1944   Yagé, planta misteriosa y sugestiva. *Colombia* 1: 6 & 7: 87–88.
Carneiro, Robert L.
    1964   The Amahuaca and the Spirit World. *Ethnology* 3: 6–11.
    n.d.   Unpublished field notes.

Chaves, Milcíades
  1958   Mítica de los Siona del alto Putumayo. *XXXI Congreso Internacional de Americanistas, Miscelanea Paul Rivet Octogenario Dictata* 2: 121–51. México: Universidad Nacional Autónoma México.

Fabre, René
  1955   Quelques plantes médicinales de l'Amérique Latine: leur utilisation thérapeutique. *Revue Générale des Sciences Pures et Appliquées (et Bulletin de l'Association Française pour l'Avancement des Sciences)* 62: 42–55. Paris.

Goldman, Irving
  1963   *The Cubeo: Indians of the Northwest Amazon.* Illinois Studies in Anthropology, No. 2. Urbana: University of Illinois Press.

Grandidier, Ernest
  1861   *Voyage dans l'Amérique du Sud: Pérou et Bolivie.* Paris: Michel Lévy Frères.

Harner, Michael J.
  1962   Jívaro Souls. *American Anthropologist* 64: 258–72.

Hissink, Karin
  1960   Notizen sur Ausbreitung des Ayahuasca-Kultes bei Chama- und Tacana-Gruppen. *Ethnologica*, neue Folge 2: 522–29. Leipzig.

Joy, Arthur, and Richard E. Schultes
  1955   Twelve Years in a Green Heaven. *Natural History* 64: 120–29. New York.

Koch-Grünberg, Theodor
  1917   *Vom Roroima zum Orinoco.* Band 1. Berlin: Dietrich Reimer.
  1923   *Zwei Jahre bei den Indianern nordwest Brasiliens.* 2nd ed. Stuttgart: Strecker und Schröder.

Mallol de Recasens, María R.
  1963   Cuatro representaciones de las imágenes alucinatorias originadas por la toma del Yagé. *Revista Colombiana de Folclor* 3(8): 59–81. Bogotá.

Oberem, Ude
  1958   Espiritus y brujos en las riberas del Napo. *Humanitas, Boletín Ecuatoriano de Antropología* 1: 76–83. Quito.

Pérez Arbeláez, Enrique
  1937   *Plantas medicinales y venenosas de Colombia.* Bogotá: Editorial "Cromos."

Plácido de Calella
   1944   Apuntes sobre los indios Sionas del Putumayo. *Anthropos*
          35–36: 737–49. Wien-Mödling.
Reichel-Dolmatoff, Gerardo
   1960   Notas etnográficas sobre los indios del Chocó. *Revista Co-
          lombiana de Antropología* 9: 73–158. Bogotá.
   1969   El contexto cultural de un alucinógeno aborigen: Banisteriop-
          sis Caapi. *Revista de la Academia Colombiana de Ciencias
          Exactas, Físicas y Naturales* 13(51): 327–45. Bogotá.
   1971   *Amazonian Cosmos: The Sexual and Religious Symbolism
          of the Tukano Indians.* Chicago and London: University of
          Chicago Press.
Reinburg, P.
   1921   Contribution a l'étude des boissons toxiques des indiens du
          nord-ouest de l'Amazonie, l'ayahuasca—le yajé—le huánto.
          Journal de la Société des Américanistes de Paris (n.s.) 13:
          25–54; 197–216. Paris.
Roessner, Tomás
   1946   El ayahuasca, planta mágica del Amazonas. *Revista Geo-
          gráfica Americana* 26: 14–16. Buenos Aires.
Santesson, C. G., and Henry Wassén
   1936   Some Observations on South American Arrow-Poisons and
          Narcotics (A Rejoinder to Professor Rafael Karsten). *Eth-
          nological Studies* 3: 330–58. Göteborg.
Spruce, Richard
   1908   *Notes of a Botanist on the Amazon and Andes* (Alfred R.
          Wallace, ed.). London: Macmillan.
Tessmann, Günter
   1930   *Die Indianer Nordost-Perus.* Hamburg: Friederichsen, de
          Gruyter and Co.
Villarejo, Avencio
   1953   *Así es la selva.* 2nd ed. Lima: Sanmartí.
Villavicencio, Manuel
   1858   *Geografía de la república del Ecuador.* New York: Robert
          Craighead.

10

Psychological Aspects of the Yagé
Experience in an Experimental Setting

Claudio Naranjo

When we consider the anthropological reports on the uses and
effects of *yagé* or *ayahuasca* among the different Indian cultures
in South America several questions naturally come to our mind:
What is peculiar to the natives' experiences or their interpretations
of such? Would a white man in our culture share what the
shamans report of themselves or would he experience the drug's
effect according to his own values, expectations, and previous life
history? In a way these questions are equivalent to asking what
kind of drug this is, since we can only generalize about the effect
of a drug seeing through and beyond personality and cultural
differences that bear on it, after which we may either affirm its
relativity or grasp a common core of experience behind the disparate interpretations and symbolizations of it in the individual
reports.

An answer to these questions, interesting to pharmacology and
psychology as well as to anthropology, can be sought in the study
of the reactions to the drug among non-natives that are not in-

CLAUDIO NARANJO, M.D., was formerly an Associate of the Institute of Personality
Assessment and Research of the University of California, Berkeley. He has conducted
experimental and clinical work in psychotherapy both at the University of Chile School
of Medicine and in the United States, to which he came as a Guggenheim fellow in
1964.

formed of the natives' accounts of theirs, so I hope that some insights in this direction can be gained from the following report on experiences from thirty-five such volunteers in Santiago, Chile. The contents of this paper will report on some features in the experience with harmaline, the active alkaloid of *yagé*, as reported by thirty-five subjects who took it either orally or by intravenous injection, in different dosage levels and in some cases more than once (*cf.* Naranjo, 1967).

I shall not go into details about the physiological aspects of the reaction or its comparison with the experience induced by other hallucinogens, but I may say that, on the one hand, the experimental subjects ingested either mescaline or LSD on a different occasion, and they all agree that their reactions to these drugs are very different from those brought about by harmaline. On the other hand, this difference partly lies in that *yagé* (or harmaline) induces a more sleep-like trance; the person under its influence generally wants to keep his eyes closed, since the external world appears as of little interest and distracting from the world of visions and inner happenings that take place when it is shut off. Parenthetically I can also mention that this trance-like state, somehow resembling sleep or a self-contained reverie, is neurophysiologically more like a state of alertness in that the EEG recordings show the disappearance of alpha waves when the subjects have their eyes closed.

But what can be of greater interest for the purpose of comparison with the preceding paper by Harner undoubtedly lies in the content of the experiences, be this the description of visions, or, in some cases, pure feelings or thoughts.

In general terms it can be said that the great majority of these experiences were of the sort that is generally misnamed hallucinatory. That is, the person would visualize with closed eyes—and rarely with open eyes—images that are not mistaken for reality (though they may be associated with intense feelings). In some of the subjects this went along with or was followed by an inclination to think about personal or metaphysical problems with a feeling of unusual depth, insight, and inspiration. In only two cases out of thirty-five a person under a full dose of the alkaloid had no hallucinations at all but only an indescribable feeling of joy, loving serenity. Most people became nauseous and some vomited profusely or experienced a vague but intense *malaise*, which on two occasions led to the interruption of the session. It is difficult to decide to what extent this discomfort was psychological in origin, but it appeared to be concomitant with a state of diminished awareness of the psychological happenings of the moment, a sort of sleepiness in which the person seemed to take refuge and shut himself off from overwhelming visions or feelings that he could not recall again.

Before we examine more closely the content of these experiences I would like it to be understood that the mere description of one such session, lasting about six hours, would easily take an hour to convey. In fact, I have in my possession a forty-page report written by one of the subjects on his experience. Since illustration with case material seems indispensable if one is to convey the particular quality of the content, in what follows I shall alternate between excerpts of session notes and the discussions of such. This will be necessarily unilateral because of the limited space available, so I have chosen to concentrate on the highlighting of some of what appear to be recurrent themes underlying the individual experiences. I think it will become apparent that almost any illustration for one of these themes could also be used to illustrate some other, since such motives converge and are condensed in a synthetic whole in the actual play of fantasy.

I have chosen as a starting point for the following discussion the first vision of a 25-year-old woman, born in Europe of European parents, who has lived in Chile since late in her childhood. She says:

> I went at a terrific speed. I came to a strange street. I only saw one side of it. It was an interminable row of two- or three-storied houses with pointed roofs and wooden beams, in the style of medieval houses or English country houses.
>
> I suddenly saw a man running. He was a messenger. I had to slow down and placed myself next to him. That is, next to his face, since in this dream only my soul participated. My soul is a sphere of some 7 cm. in diameter, pure energy, and it rotates on itself at such enormous speed that it would be the same if it didn't. It can displace itself in any direction at the speed it

wishes. My soul sees, hears, thinks; it perceives odors, I believe, but has no sense of touch for the simple reason that it repels matter.

We must in the first place take notice that this is a dream of fantasy of her "soul," and this awareness of an entity which is regarded as a soul as distinct from the body is seen with the same explicitness in other experiences too. Consider the following description by a 21-year-old Chilean journalist:

> I was going farther and farther away from myself. I was realizing that my body and my mind were such autonomous forces that if they had ever converged in me it seemed pure chance. What during my entire lifetime I had sensed like mingled confusion now appeared to be divided in three precise domains: outside lay the world, people, buildings and noises (for which I cared less and less); closer, as a boundary, stood my organism, with those hands, that mouth and its laugh, now commanded by itself; inside, at last, in the innermost and recondite, warmly floating in the skin that was always with me, was I. That is, my mind.

It is perhaps this transition from everyday-like awareness to that of the autonomous self, soul, mind, or whatever name we may wish to call it, that might perhaps explain recurrent images of falling into one's body, or simply falling—leaving the everyday ground —entering one's body or some symbolic place. The process is also expressed as one of dissociating and leaving, as going unconscious (though this does not actually happen) or, more radically, dying. Eight persons in thirty-five experienced visions or feelings of their own death.

The same subject of the last quotation felt he was dying, too, and comments: "If I was going to leave the body, that didn't worry me. I knew that I existed in essence, and this was the ideal state, with no skin, no liver, no resentments, atemporal."

In one of the two subjects who did not visualize, the experience of death was present too, but as pure feeling and as a bodily sensation: "Physically I felt that I was dying and I feel that when my time comes I shall die well."

In the following excerpt both the theme of death and that of an independent soul can be noticed:

I saw my own death, with anguish; how I was carried across fields of rice in Korea or China, on a stretcher, between two men, coolies, perhaps, and I could see my face, once more from the outside and very close. It was like tanned leather, as in a suitcase, covered with droplets of blood or scratches on the temples. . . .

The observer in this scene is a point in space, and the subject has previously commented that there is a feeling to it like being a butterfly. But this can now lead us to a different theme.

If we now turn our attention once more to the image of that spherical soul flying at high speed I would like to point out that this speed itself tends to recur in other visions; the lack of tactile sensations perhaps has its equivalence in a feeling of benumbedness which is often reported, whereas its being suspended in space, soaring through it at some altitude appears or is implied in about one-third of the subjects' comments or reports.

Consider the following excerpt from the account of a male subject who took a fairly large amount of harmaline with the addition of mescaline:

The first thing I did, involuntarily, was lift my hand. It seemed to lose weight, it rose, rose . . . and then I felt that it was no longer a hand but the tip of a wing. I was turning into a winged being. I then stretched my wings and felt extreme freedom and expansion. My wings were growing and as they did my feeling of freedom increased, as if I had been imprisoned during my entire lifetime and I suddenly had organs that made it possible for me to expand. And I would say: "I have wings! I have wings! There is no space that can contain them, the air cannot contain them, they are immense!" I felt my wings grow above the earth, and had the image of a huge bird above the earth, with its extended wings beyond its limits, reaching infinity. I then, timidly, began to move them. I felt the movements of flying clearly: how the wing rested on the resisting air, and how a wave of motion went from the tip to the other end permitting me to lift the body. And I said: "I fly! I fly!" And felt the air coming into my mouth, caressing my whole body, and saw the perspective of the earth. I didn't go anywhere. I just flew and the air passing through my body gave my breathing a special rhythm, a rhythm of flying which expressed not only the movement but the joy.

It may be related to this experience of flying that some subjects who do not report it as such nevertheless describe their visions as scenes viewed from above, sometimes from great altitude. Such evidence of an aerial viewpoint can be found, for example, in the following description:

> I remember a Negro woman I saw from above . . . I saw her from a distance of some 3 meters and then approached her further, from her right side. She carried a purple parasol of a very bright, almost luminous color, like a sea anemone, like embroidery, and would twist it around its axis so that it unfolded like loose chiffon or in the form of an aurora borealis, and she laughed with a coarse and vulgar laugh.

It happens with this as with many other *yagé* visions that it contains more than one of the recurrent themes, and I would be tempted to elaborate on each. Here it is not only the physical point of view from above that seems typical but, too, the image of a geometric center for the happenings, the merry-go-round-like rotation, the Negro woman and the experience of being teased. For the time being I shall conclude the discussion of the flight-theme by mentioning the most common presentation of it, which is the mere visualization of birds. The following is not the most typical example, but may be interesting from many points of view:

> Suddenly, a crucified Christ ascended moving his arms like wings. And then another, moving his arms with the crossed sticks. All these movements were at an incredible speed. I thought, in seeing it, that here was from where the idea had come of depicting the Holy Ghost as a dove. And then Christ turned into a sort of dove that ascended.

On the whole ten subjects mentioned at least one of the experiences related to flying.

I would now like to concentrate on another aspect of our initial quotation, which is the spherical shape and rotating motion of the transparent flying sphere. I am mentioning both the rotation and the shape not only because the first already suggests the idea of circularity, but for the fact that both, in turn, imply the idea of a center of the form or movement. This center may be the most adequate symbol to refer to the theme we now want to discuss.

It may be recalled that this idea of a central element and the rotating motion were already encountered in that vision of the Negro woman with the turning parasol which unfolded into an aurora borealis. Now consider the following passage from the same person's report:

> I saw tiny dots, like those on a television screen, transparent dots that agitated and turned (when I fixed the gaze on one point) around a cone forming a sort of funnel, like the whirlpool that is formed when one removes the stopper. They turned, rather slowly, and this funnel opened upwards from the floor I was gazing at, and extended to the sides into my entire visual field. . . . And in this swirl of particles lies all my visual experience. It all comes from it, this is the foundation of the scenes I saw, this was their spirit, in the same way that the dots on the television screen are the ground of all the images; but even the meaning of this incessant turning was in everything, like a merry-go-round, or like fair-music; it *was* like circus music. Was the teasing already here? Something of a sardonic joke was in all of this, these changing situations confronting the spectator (me), these images in incessant transformation, never permanent, meaning nothing but change as such, like the whirlpool that turned and carried in it all these visions.

[Compare this account with the drawing by a Jívaro Indian in Fig. V in the previous chapter. Ed.]

The "center" can appear in the different visions as a source of motion or the region to which motion flows, a source of light or a perceiving eye, a geometric region such as a circular pond in the middle of Heaven or Hell, a being at the center of the earth, of the universe, the skull or inside the subject's body. (In nine of the subjects this was a noticeable feature appearing in more than one image.) From the subject's experiences and associations, as from the context in which these images appear, I definitely believe that this contraposition of center and periphery, the core and the surface, the immobile and the incessant turning, the source, beginning and end, and the everchanging flow, is that of the deeper self and the multiplicity of experience, and it encompasses but transcends the duality of mind and body. More precisely, it is that of being and becoming, and it matches the traditional Hindu symbol for *samsāra* and *nirvāna:* the wheel of incessant death and rebirth, and its hub. Or, according to a remarkable passage of the *tao-tê-ching*, the practical materiality of a jar and the enclosed void that constitutes its essence.

I still have to illustrate one of the most important and striking themes in the *yagé* experiences, but this time, if I am to illustrate it with the initial dream of the spherical soul I have to quote a bit further from it. After describing the messenger in what seems to be medieval clothes, the subject goes on:

I left him behind and proceeded onwards, skimming just above the ground. I met a very large man, a sort of giant with a bronzed skin, black moustache, leather jacket and pants made of leopard's skin, who looked at me in a rage, who knows why. He produced a very long whip and wanted to whip me with it, taking my soul for a top. But the whip would stop at one cm. from my soul and couldn't go further. The giant and the whip were furious about their failure. The whip then turned into a black serpent's head with no teeth, that opened its mouth wanting to devour me. It could not. At the moment my soul's attention was caught by a funeral procession so I didn't see the giant or the whip anymore.

So here we find, in a brief scene, rage, dark skin, hostile whipping, leopard skin, a black serpent, and the prospect of being swallowed. In this particular instance, too, the soul appears invulnerable to the threats because of its very nature. Here, as in other instances, it can be a matter of choice how embracing a category we want to regard as a theme. Serpents certainly recur in the visions, and crocodiles or reptiles in general, and so do tigers, leopards and cats; but fangs also do, and birds of prey and vampires, and perhaps all these are interrelated by their implication of danger, and would also be related to the giant and the whip. Since it is not possible in the present circumstances to elaborate on the different elements of this complex, though, I shall choose to illustrate the two which are striking enough at least for their frequency. Strangely enough, tigers, leopards, or jaguars were seen by seven of the subjects even though big cats are not seen in Chile. These are sometimes encountered as aggressors, sometimes as a graceful sight, a friendly companion or, in one instance, experienced as a true impersonation. Reptiles, too, were seen by six subjects. In three instances these were dragons, and in another there was a dinosaur. Snakes were reported by three subjects, and for one of them these were the most prominent element in the whole experience.

The following excerpt is from the same lady of the spherical soul and the giant with the leopard skin:

> At first, many tiger faces. Panthers and all kinds of cats. Black and yellow. Then *the* tiger. The largest and strongest of all. I know (for I read his thought) that I must follow him. I see the plateau. He walks with resolution in a straight line. I follow; but on reaching the edge and perceiving the brightness I cannot follow him. The dream vanishes. But above the luminescence rises a statue of the Virgin with the child in her arms, and ascends from the hole into the sky.

At a still later stage she is able to follow the tiger further to the end of the plateau and look into the abyss which is Hell (see Fig. I). It is round and in it is fluid fire, or fluid gold. People swim in it.

> The tiger wants me to go there. I don't know how to descend. I grasp the tiger's tail and he jumps. Because of his musculature the jump is graceful and slow. The tiger swims in the liquid fire as I sit on his back. I then suddenly see my tiger is eating up a woman. But no. It is not the tiger. It is an animal with a crocodile's head and the body of a fatter, larger animal with four feet (though these were not seen). All kinds of lizards and frogs begin to appear now. And the pond gradually turns into a greenish swamp of stagnant waters, though full of life: primitive forms of life, such as algae, anemones, and micro-organisms. It is a prehistoric pond [see Fig. II]. A shore appears, not with sand but vegetation. Some dinosaurs are seen in the distance. I rise on the tiger on the shore. The serpent follows us. It catches up with us. I stay aside and let the tiger take care of her [see Fig. III]. But the serpent is strong and my tiger is in danger. I decide to take part in the fight. The serpent notices my intention, lets the tiger loose and prepares to attack us. I hold its head and press on its sides so that it will open its mouth. It has an iron-piece inside, like the bit of a horse. I press on the ends of this bit and the serpent dies or disintegrates, it falls into pieces as if it were a mechanical serpent. I go onwards with the tiger. I walk next to him, my arm over his neck. We climb

the high mountain. There is a zig-zag path between high bushes. We arrive. There is a crater. We wait for some time and there begins an enormous eruption. The tiger tells me I must throw myself into the crater. I am sad to leave my companion but I know that this last journey I must travel. I throw myself into the fire that comes out of the crater. I ascend with the flames towards the sky and fly onwards.

I have deliberately quoted more than what is strictly relevant to the mere illustration of the tiger motive so at least an intuition can be formed as to the complex relationships between the themes of tiger, serpent, crocodile, fire, destruction, and those of flying, ascending, disembodied existence.

Just one more example before we proceed to a different aspect, this time from the same person who felt like a huge bird flying beyond the limits of the earth:

I wasn't a fish anymore, but a big cat, a tiger. I walked, though, feeling the same freedom I had experienced as a bird and a fish, freedom of movement, flexibility, grace. I moved as a tiger in the jungle, joyously, feeling the ground under my feet, feeling my power; my chest grew larger. I then approached an animal, any animal. I only saw its neck, and then experienced what a tiger feels when looking at its prey.

This may be enough to show how the tiger by no means stands for mere hostility, but for a fluid synthesis of aggression and grace and a full acceptance of the life-impulse beyond moral judgment.

It is now time to turn to an aspect in these experiences which is much more diversified than those discussed, and which, though expressed here and there through particularized images, can choose such a variety of images that it makes it more appropriate to speak of a trait or quality of the *yagé* experience than of a "theme." This quality is what we may want to call the religious or the mythical.

If we choose to regard as religious those images which belong in this category according to common knowledge, or the feelings and concerns that the subjects express in explicitly religious terms, we find that these were reported by fifteen out of the thirty-five. Five persons saw the Devil or devils, three of them mentioned angels, three had a vision of the Virgin Mary and two of Christ;

I. Hell

II. Hell transformed into a primeval swamp

III. The subject's tiger guardian fights a serpent

three spoke of Paradise or Heaven, and two of Hell, three of them described priestly figures, while others saw churches, altars, or crosses. Aside from these fifteen, two had ecstatic feelings which were described in religious terms.

It is probably an arbitrary matter where to trace the limit between what is religious and what is not. One instance of this can be seen in the transition between the vision of "the Devil" or minor demons to monstrous images or horrible masks, and from these to horrible people or animals. References to Greco-Roman gods, sirens or nymphs are not uncommon, and we may wish to place them in the same category with the religious images of Christianity. And, again, we can detect a mythical quality in the atmosphere of the typical fairy tale, with castles, kings, and medieval costumes, as has been reported in at least four of the experiences. One subject said he felt like a pharaoh, but in his written report two days later he did not mention the image or idea of a pharaoh, but said instead that this was a feeling of being God. If it were not for this additional information, the essential religious implication of the image could have been overlooked. For these reasons I believe the mythico-religious element is more pervasive in the experiences than what appears from their outward descriptions and may be completely unrelated to the visual imagery. In one instance, for example, a subject had been instructed to imagine the depth of the ocean. Only a month later did I discover, to my own surprise, the importance that this experience had for her:

> The most important was descending to the bottom of the sea [she commented]. The feeling of being myself. The sea was in myself. There was a continuity of the external with the internal. I have recalled this when I have been unhappy. The sand and the plants were myself or something of mine. The idea of God was in everything. I think that must be what is called a mystical experience. I cannot describe it. I wouldn't have words. Beauty, joy, peace, everything I longed for was there. God in myself.

A familiar mythical character came to the fore during an experience the most important aspect of which was the feeling the subject had of not being the doer of his actions when he talked, laughed, or made a drawing. When he looked at himself in a mirror, too, his face seemed to him a mask while somebody else was looking through his eyes. This feeling of being, so to say, "possessed" by another spirit developed into the notion that this was a dwarf inside of him. This dwarf, childlike and aged at the same time, bisexual or asexual, manipulator of the body and free from necessity but, at the same time imprisoned by the body, was part of his perception of different situations during the drug experience, and the following excerpt refers to his viewing of a picture showing a sexual act:

. . . I thought eroticism would come next but it didn't. Never did I grasp the carnal side of the movements, and I saw it as an act as natural as any. Then, what was physically a genital turned into a communication tube, a bridge between two beings. The figures were communicating in the only possible way, interrupting during a fleeting interval the solitude of the spirit. Then, suddenly, the dwarf appeared in the bodies, laughing in amusement while he pushed out his obscene finger. He took delight in it since this was his definitive, triumphant joke: while the body believed it was seeking its satisfaction it was really letting free the imprisoned dwarf. Love, it seemed, was the supreme irony. Man and woman give themselves to each other in pleasure, the body instinctively seeks it, but, in the accomplishment, it ceases to exist, since the orgasm is a fleeting death. It being death, imprisonment and dependency cease to exist. In the battle between the body and the dwarf this was the truce. But suddenly the dwarf's laughter vanished, and as if it were sucked by itself it grew smaller and smaller until it was only a light, an incandescent worm, a shining point, a microscopic and luminous spermatozoan. In this state it shot from the man's body to the woman's womb. In the midst of this truce the dwarf, too, was fooled. He was forced to abandon his inaction and was precipitated into doing something. A new human being, to begin again the cycle with the duality of dwarf and body. This led me to the thought of a higher joke.

Even though the focus of this report has been descriptive, I think the different motives illustrated thus far almost out of their own accord fall together in an embracing whole. The complex of images discussed first as portraying the polarity of being and becoming, freedom and necessity, spirit and matter, only set up the stage for the human drama. This involves the battle of opposites and eventually their reconciliation or fusion, after giving way to death and destruction, be this by fire, tigers, drowning, or devouring snakes. The beauty of fluid fire, the graceful tiger, or the subtle and wise reptile, these seem most expressive for the synthetic experience of accepting life as a whole, or, better, accepting existence as a whole, life and death included; evil included too, though from a given spiritual perspective it is not experienced as evil any more. Needless to say, the process is essentially religious, and it could even be suspected that every myth presents us one particular aspect of the same experience.

The themes I have illustrated are by no means the only ones that can be discerned in the sessions. As I mentioned in passing, Negro people appear very frequently, and this research was carried out in Chile where there are no Negroes. Landscapes and cities are often described (as the medieval houses in the first quotation) and these sometimes seem to be related to the experience of flying. Masks, especially monstrous or sardonic ones are often mentioned, and so are eyes. Not uncommonly robots, vehicles or a feeling of automation are reported, and so are mobs, caves, prehistory, pearls, and so on. It would take too long to illustrate all of them and more so to elaborate on their meaning. I think, though, that the themes discussed here are the central ones, and I would suggest that they invite us to regard some shamanistic conceptions more as the expression of universal experiences than in terms of acculturation to local traditions.

REFERENCE

Naranjo, Claudio
1967   Psychotropic Properties of the Harmala Alkaloids. In *Ethnopharmacologic Search for Psychoactive Drugs* (Daniel H. Efron, editor-in-chief), pp. 385–91. Public Health Service Publication No. 1645. Washington, D.C.: U.S. Department of Health, Education and Welfare.

General Bibliography

Aberle, David F.
1966   *The Peyote Religion among the Navaho*. Chicago: Aldine.
Agurell, S., B. Holmstedt, and J. E. Lindgren
1968   Alkaloid Content of Banisteriopsis Rusbyana. *American Journal of Pharmacy* 140: 148–51.

Carneiro, Robert L.
1964   The Amahuaca and the Spirit World. *Ethnology* 3: 6–11.

Castaneda, Carlos
1968   *The Teachings of Don Juan: A Yaqui Way of Knowledge*. Berkeley and Los Angeles: University of California Press.
1971   *A Separate Reality: Further Conversations with Don Juan*. New York: Simon and Schuster.

Der Marderosian, Ara H., Kenneth M. Kensinger, Jew-ming Chao, and Frederick J. Goldstein
1970   The Use and Hallucinatory Principles of a Psychoactive Beverage of the Cashinahua Tribe (Amazon Basin). *Drug Dependence* No. 5: 7–14. Chevy Chase, Maryland: National Institute of Health.

Dobkin de Rios, Marlene
1972   *Visionary Vine: Psychedelic Healing in the Peruvian Amazon*. San Francisco: Chandler.

Durkheim, Emile
1965   *The Elementary Forms of the Religious Life*. New York: Free Press. Original French edition, 1912.

Eliade, Mircea
1964   *Shamanism: Archaic Techniques of Ecstasy.* Bollingen Series
       LXXVI. New York: Pantheon.
Eugster, Conrad H.
1967   Isolation, Structure and Synthesis of Central-Active Com-
       pounds from Amanita Muscaria (L. ex. F) Hooker. In
       Ethnopharmacologic Search for Psychoactive Drugs (Daniel
       H. Efron, editor-in-chief), pp. 416–18. Public Health Serv-
       ice Publication No. 1645. Washington, D.C.: U.S. Depart-
       ment of Health, Education and Welfare.
Farnsworth, Norman R.
1968   Hallucinogenic Plants. *Science* 162: 1086–92.
Friedberg, Claudine
1965   Des Banisteriopsis utilisés comme drogue en Amérique du
       Sud. *Journal d'Agriculture Tropicale et de Botanique Appli-
       quée* 12: 9–12.
Furst, Peter T. (editor)
1972   *Flesh of the Gods: The Ritual Use of Hallucinogens.* New
       York: Praeger.
Harner, Michael J.
1972   *The Jívaro: People of the Sacred Waterfalls.* New York:
       Doubleday/Natural History Press.
Heim, Roger
1963   *Les Champignons toxiques et hallucinogènes.* Paris: N.
       Boubée.
Hoffer, A., and H. Osmund
1967   *The Hallucinogens.* New York and London: Academic Press.
Jochelson, Waldemar I.
1905– *The Koryak. Report of the Jessup Expedition,* 1900–1901.
1908   Memoirs of the American Museum of Natural History, vol.
       10, part 2. New York.
La Barre, Weston
1938   *The Peyote Cult.* Yale University Publications in Anthro-
       pology, No. 19. New Haven.
1960   Twenty Years of Peyote Studies. *Current Anthropology*
       1: 45–60.
1969   *The Peyote Cult.* Enlarged edition. New York: Schocken
       Books.
Lewin, Louis
1964   *Phantastica, Narcotic and Stimulating Drugs: Their Use
       and Abuse.* Translated from the second German edition.
       New York: E. P. Dutton. Original German edition, 1924.

Lewis, I. M.
  1971 *Ecstatic Religion: An Anthropological Study of Spirit Posses-sion and Shamanism.* Middlesex: Penguin.

Morton, C. V.
  1930 Notes on Yagé, a Drug Plant of Southeastern Colombia. *Journal of the Washington Academy of Sciences* 21: 485–88.

Pinkley, Homer V.
  1969 Plant Admixtures to *Ayahuasca*, the South American Hallu-cinogenic Drink. *Lloydia* 32: 305–14.

Poisson, J.
  1965 Note sur le "Natem," boisson toxique péruvienne et ses al-caloïdes. *Annales Pharmaceutiques Françaises* 23: 241–44.

Porta, Giovanni Battista [John Baptista Porta]
  1658 *Natural Magick.* Translated from the expurgated Italian edition of 1589. Reproduction of the 1658 English edition. New York: Basic Books. 1957.

Schultes, Richard E.
  1940 Teonanacatl: Narcotic Mushrooms of the Aztecs. *American Anthropologist* 42: 429–43.
  1955 A New Narcotic Genus from the Amazon Slope of the Colombian Andes. *Botanical Museum Leaflets*, Harvard Uni-versity, 17: 1–11.
  1957 The Identity of the Malpighiaceous Narcotics of South America. *Botanical Museum Leaflets*, Harvard University, 18 (1).
  1960 Pharmacognosy. *The Pharmaceutical Sciences* [Third Lecture Series, 1960], part 5: 138–85.
  1963 Botanical Sources of the New World Narcotics. *Psychedelic Review* 1: 145–66.
  1970 The Botanical and Chemical Distribution of Hallucinogens. *Annual Review of Plant Physiology* 21: 571–98. Palo Alto.

Slotkin, James S.
  1956 *The Peyote Religion.* Glencoe, Ill.: Free Press.

Spruce, Richard
  1908 *Notes of a Botanist on the Amazon and Andes* (Alfred R. Wallace, ed.). London: Macmillan.

Standley, Paul C., and Julian A. Steyermark
  1946 Flora of Guatemala. *Fieldiana: Botany*, vol. 24, part 5. Chicago.

Stevenson, Matilda C.
  1915 Ethnobotany of the Zuñi Indians. *Thirtieth Annual Report*

of the Bureau of American Ethnology to the Secretary of the Smithsonian Institution, 1908–1909, pp. 31–102. Washington, D.C.

Tylor, Edward B.

1924   *Primitive Culture: Researches into the Development of Mythology, Philosophy, Religion, Language, Art, and Custom.* 2 vols. (combined). New York: Brentano's. Originally published 1871.

Waser, Peter G.

1967   The Pharmacology of Amanita Muscaria. In *Ethnopharmacologic Search for Psychoactive Drugs* (Daniel H. Efron, editor-in-chief), pp. 419–39.

Wasson, R. Gordon

1958   The Divine Mushroom: Primitive Religion and Hallucinatory Agents. *Proceedings of the American Philosophical Society* 102: 221–23.

1961   The Hallucinogenic Fungi of Mexico: An Inquiry into the Origins of the Religious Idea among Primitive Peoples. *Botanical Museum Leaflets*, Harvard University, 19: 137–62.

1968   *Soma, Divine Mushroom of Immortality.* Ethno-Mycological Studies, No. 1. New York: Harcourt, Brace and World.

Wasson, R. Gordon, and Roger Heim

1958   *Les Champignons hallucinogènes du Mexique.* Paris: Muséum National d'Histoire Naturelle.

Wasson, R. Gordon, and Valentina P. Wasson

1957   *Mushrooms, Russia and History.* 2 vols. New York: Pantheon Books.

Index